ENGINE & DRIVETRAIN

Performance MATH

For street & race track applications

Over 65 Solved Problems!

STATIC & DYNAMIC COMPRESSION RATIOS!

FIRST EDITION

Volume One

by **Vincent W. Robinson**
Mechanical Engineer

Engine & Drivetrain Performance Math (Volume 1) -- First Edition

Author: Vincent W. Robinson

ISBN: 0-9643024-7-0

ISBN: 978-0-9643024-7-1

Part Number: RP-134

Copyright © Vincent W. Robinson, 2003

All rights reserved. No part of this publication may be stored in a retrieval system, transmitted or reproduced in any way, form, or by any means. This includes, but is not limited to photographs, photocopying, electronic, magnetic, or other recording methods, without any verbal agreement and written permission of the publisher.

The information herein this book is true and complete to the best of my knowledge. Any recommendation(s) and / or reference(s) to any parts, procedures, data, or knowledge are made without any guarantee(s) on the part of the author or publisher. The author and publisher disclaims all liability incurred in connection with the use of this information or material.

Cover photographs: They are courtesy of Chevrolet Motorsports, Jerico Performance Products, and Precision Gear.

Publisher: Robinson Publishing
Alcoa, Tennessee 37701-2213

Web site: www.enginemath.com
E-Mail: robinsonpublishing@enginemath.com

Printed in the United States of America

Revised – 02/2014

Table Of Contents

- Preface v
- Chapter-1   Cylinder Block Deck Height 1
- Chapter-2   Engine Displacement 5
- Chapter-3   Bore - To - Stroke Ratio 7
- Chapter-4   Rod - To - Stroke Ratio 9
- Chapter-5   Rod Angularity 11
- Chapter-6   Piston Displacement 15
- Chapter-7   Cylinder Volume - Versus - Crank Angle 31
- Chapter-8   Average Piston Speed 39
- Chapter-9   Instantaneous Piston Speed 45
- Chapter-10 Static Compression Ratio 61
- Chapter-11 Dynamic Compression Ratio 65
- Chapter-12 Air Mass Efficiency 69
- Chapter-13 Brake Mean Effective Pressure(BMEP) 75
- Chapter-14 Brake Torque 79
- Chapter-15 Power / Horsepower / Brake Horsepower 83
- Chapter-16 CAMSHAFTS(Principles, Valve Timing, & Valve Events) .. 87
- Chapter-17 Carburetor Air Flow 99
- Chapter-18 Drivetrain -- Overall Gear Ratios 103
- Chapter-19 Transmission -- Output Shaft Speed 109
- Chapter-20 Rear End -- Axle Speed 111
- Chapter-21 Maximum -- Vehicle Speed 113
-
- Abbreviations 117
- Conversions 121
- Glossary 123

Engine & Drivetrain Performance Math (Volume 1)

Engine & Drivetrain Performance Math (Volume 1)

Engine & Drivetrain Performance Math (Volume 1)

PREFACE

PURPOSE

THE PRIMARY INTENT OF this Engine & Drivetrain Performance Math manual is to establish a mathematical approach to solving problems associated with the four stroke internal combustion engine and its associated drivetrain incorporating rear wheel drive. In conjuction with the above approach, its intent is also to provide the reader with some practical and some theoretical background knowledge underlying these problems.

APPLICATIONS

The information in this book primarily covers engine parameters, specifications, torque, horsepower, camshafts, air mass efficiency, carburetor air flow rates; overall gear ratios; and also transmission, rear end and vehicle speeds.

This information can be used for any related vehicle on the street, drag strip, road racing course, dirt track, water, mud racing, sand racing, or asphalt racing track; such as: cars, trucks, motorcycles, boats, and any mechanical application that uses either a four stroke internal combustion engine, manual or automatic transmission, a conventional rear end, or any *combination* of these three elements.

PERSPECTIVE

MANY "rules of thumb" methods are often used in engine building and setting up drivetrain gear ratios. This book provides a mathematical approach to solving these problems. You don't have to know algebra or trigonometry to solve the problems in this book. Just follow the examples shown and substitute any practical data into the desired equation(s). All you may need is a simple arithmetic calculator, or a scientific calculator can be used for some equations and/or trigonometric functions to make it much simpler to perform some calculations. Also, the equations and information in this book may be used to complement any related computer programs, and other related internal combustion engine and drivetrain material.

MATERIAL FOUNDATION

ALL MATTER BEHAVES ACCORDING TO the physical laws that were discovered by Isaac Newton. The principles, equations, and solved problems in this book are based very much on this foundation. This also includes any related geometry that's associated with this matter.

BASIS OF DESIRED EFFECTS

THE EFFECTIVENESS OF THE results that you will achieve from the use of this information will depend highly upon the accuracy of the data that you use to insert into the equations, and to what extent a person dedicates themselves to thinking through a particular engine and/or drivetrain combination.

FEATURES

This book includes many features that should make it easy for the inexperienced/experienced engine and drivetrain builders to use:

- **Principles** -- The basic physical laws concerning the operation of each mechanical part. These laws are used to analyze and/or explain the function of each part or process.

PREFACE

- **Equations --**
Presented in order to calculate the various parameters when any practical data is given

- **Bold line around an equation --** Indicates that it is a *major equation* used to calculate a final result

- **Thin line around an equation --** Indicates that it is a *necessary equation* that has to be used prior to the major equation or it is given for information only

- **Example problems --** Are given to explain and familiarize the user with the use of each equation

- **Data --** Information made available to make it easier for the user to solve any related problems

- **Graph(s) --** Given in order to show the relationship between two or more pieces of data

- **Illustrations / Diagrams --** To clarify or explain by using examples or comparisons

- **Photographs --** For exhibition purposes or to help provide additional information about a subject(s)

- **Tables --** To show the relationship between related data and to provide data for substitution into any applicable equation(s)

- **Abbreviations --** To reduce word length, and to make each word or words more easily recognizable *(one or more abbreviations are sometimes used to represent more than one thing)*

- **Conversions --** They are used to convert a number from one unit of measure to another unit of measure

- **Glossary --** A definition of the terms used in this book

SUPPLEMENTARY INFORMATION

EACH CHAPTER BEGINS on the right side of this book for simplicity. This is so that the beginning of each chapter can be easily found and easily read when looking or thumbing through it.

AT THE END OF SOME chapters in this book, the last page is left blank intentionally. These pages are titled "Calculations", and can be used for manual calculations.

CHAPTER 1

CYLINDER BLOCK DECK HEIGHT

THE ENGINE'S *DECK HEIGHT (Dk Ht)* *IS* defined as the distance from the centerline of the crank to the crown of the block as shown in *Figure 1-1*. The component parameters included in this stack-up are: the crank throw-r, the connecting rod's length-R(measured from the center of the connecting rod's crank journal to the center of the connecting rod's piston pin journal), the piston's compression height-c, and the deck height's clearance-D, if any.

THE TOTAL LENGTH OF all components along the cylinder bore's centerline, should'nt exceed the cylinder block's deck height when assembled.

ADDITIONAL PHOTOGRAPHS REVEALING THESE internal components(the connecting rod assemblies) and an engine's cylinder block parameters are shown in **Figure 1-3** & **Figure 1-4**.

THEREFORE, the equation for an engine's deck height is given by:

- Dk Ht -- Deck Height
- D -- Dk Ht Clearance
- c -- Piston Pin Height
- R -- Connecting Rod length(from center of big end - to - center of small end)
- r -- Crank Throw (from center of main journal - to - center of rod journal)

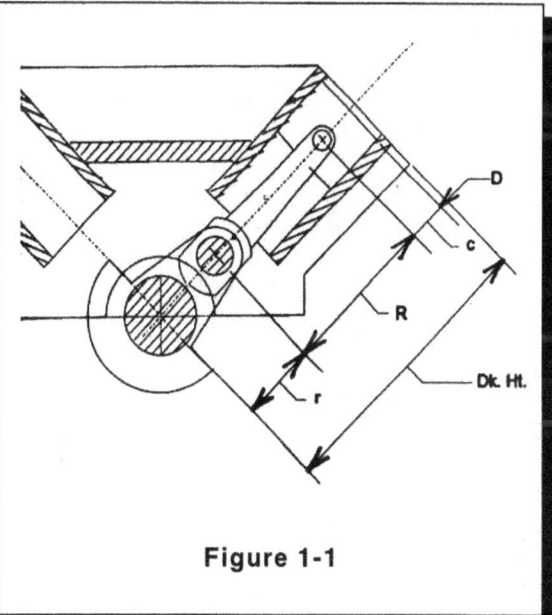

Figure 1-1

$$Dk\ Ht = D + c + R + r$$

The following photograghs of *Figure 1-2* and *Figure 1-3* reveals a view of an engine's internal components for a connecting rod assembly, and internal parameters of an engine(s) main journals and cylinder bores.

Figure 1-2: A Piston is in proximity to the top(deck) of the block; pistons & pins are shown; rods are connected to the piston pins and crankshaft's rod journals; and the crank's main journals are exposed.
Photograph -- Is courtesy of GM Performance Parts.

Figure 1-3: The crankshaft's main journal locations are marked by the five circles formed by the main bearing caps bolted to the block.
Photograph -- Is courtesy of GM Performance Parts.

Figure 1-4: Note this inverted view of the crankshaft's main journal location relative to the top(deck) of the cylinder bore.
Photograph -- Is courtesy of GM Performance Parts.

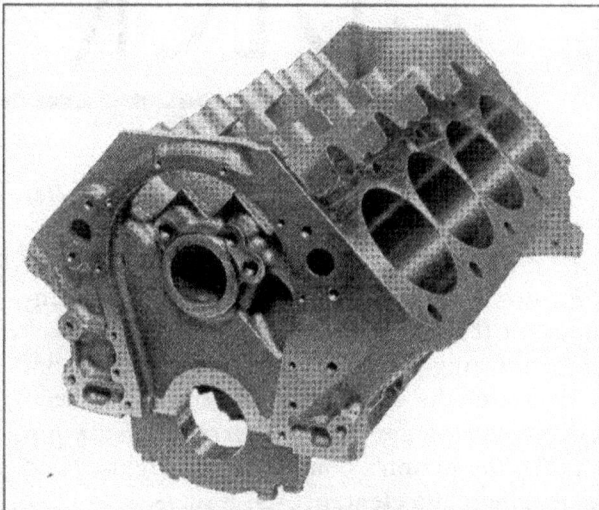

Figure 1-5: This is an upright view of an engine's cylinder block showing the deck of the cylinder bores relative to the crankshaft's main journal location.
Photograph -- Is courtesy of GM Performance Parts.

EXAMPLE(1a):
For a 3.00" stroke, a 5.7" rod length, a 1.4" piston pin height, and deck height clearance of .0135", the engine block's deck height will be...

$$Dk\ Ht = D + c + R + r$$

$r = \text{Stroke}/2$

$\text{Dk Ht} = .0135" + 1.4" + 5.7" + \dfrac{3.00"}{2}$

$\text{Dk Ht} = .0135" + 1.4" + 5.7" + 1.50"$

$\text{Dk Ht} = 8.6135"$

EXAMPLE(1b):
Let's say your engine's deck height is 10.5 inches -- This means that <u>D + c + R + r</u> - that is in Figure 1-1 - should not be greater than 10.5".
For: c = 1.825", R = 6.658", and r = 2.0", the <u>Dk Ht Clearance</u> can be computed by...

Substituting the data given above into the following equation yields...

$\boxed{D = \text{Dk Ht} - c - R - r}$

$D = 10.5" - 1.825" - 6.658" - 2.0"$

$D = 10.5" - 1.825" - 8.658"$

$D = 10.5" - 10.483"$

$D = .017"$ (Deck Height Clearance)

- Since there remains a .017" clearance, this indicates that the deck height has not been exceeded.

- If **D** were equal to zero, this would mean that the total components' dimensions are equal to the deck height.

If **D** were **negative or minus(-)**, this would indicate that the total components' dimensions are greater than the deck height, and therefore, should be reduced to avoid any possible engine damage.

CALCULATIONS

CHAPTER 2

ENGINE DISPLACEMENT

THE TERM **"Engine Displacement"** -- piston displacement -- is synonymous with the term "Swept Volume" or maximum "Swept volume" in this case. This is the volume that remains above the piston after it travels from Top Dead Center(TDC) to Bottom Dead Center(BDC), or the volume displaced after the piston moves from BDC to TDC -- resulting from one stroke of the crankshaft -- multiplied times the number of cylinders(see Figure 2-1). The principles of the engine's displacement are based upon the following information. First, the area of the cylinder, **Area = PI x (D^2/4)**; where **PI**(pronounced - pie) = **3.14159** (*This is the ratio of the circumference(C) of a circle to its diameter(D)*, that is, **PI = C/D**). This ratio is *constant* for any circle regardless of its circumference and diameter!

HENCE, INFORMATION REGARDING THE engine's cylinder area is follows:

So, the area of the cylinder, **Cylinder Area = PI x (Bore Diameter^2/4)**; and, **PI = Bore Circumference / Bore Diameter**).

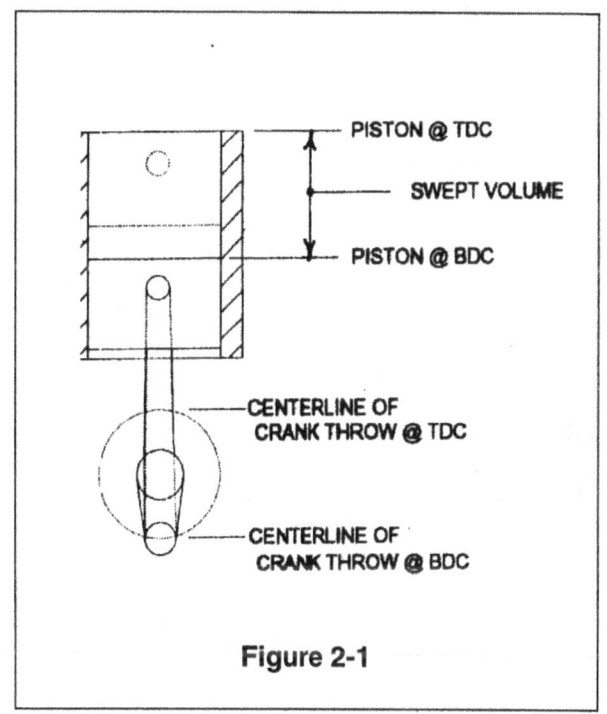

Figure 2-1

$$\text{Cylinder Area} = 3.14159 \times \frac{\text{Bore}^2}{4}$$

NEXT, THE displaced cylinder volume or swept volume per cylinder is determined by using the following equation:

> Cylinder Volume = Cylinder Area x Stroke

THE TOTAL ENGINE DISPLACEMENT IS DETERMINED BY multiplying the engine's cylinder volume times the total number of cylinders in the cylinder block.

Total Eng Displ -- Total Engine Displacement
Cylinder Vol -- Cylinder Volume
No. of Cyl -- Number of Cylinders

Therefore,

> Total Eng Displ = Cylinder Vol x No. of Cyl

EXAMPLE(2a):
Let's consider an engine with a bore equal to 4 inches, and a stroke of 3.48 inches. With these variables, the cylinder volume for <u>one</u> cylinder will be...

First,

> Cylinder Area = $3.14159 \times \dfrac{Bore^2}{4}$

Cylinder Area = $3.14159 \times \dfrac{(4\ in)^2}{4}$

Cylinder Area = $3.14159 \times \dfrac{4\ in \times 4\ in}{4}$

Cylinder Area = $3.14159 \times \dfrac{16\ in^2}{4}$

Cylinder Area = $3.14159 \times 4\ in^2$

Cylinder Area = $12.56636\ in^2$

Hence,

> Cylinder Volume = Cylinder Area x Stroke

Cylinder Volume = $12.56636\ in^2 \times 3.48\ in$

Cylinder Volume = <u>43.73</u>09328 in^3

Cylinder Volume = 43.73 cu in (rounded off)

EXAMPLE(2b):
For an 8 cylinder engine, substitute the calculated cylinder volume from Example(2a), and the total cylinder volume will be...

> Total Eng Displ = Cylinder Vol x No. of Cyl

Total Eng Displ = $43.73\ in^3 \times$ 8 cylinders

Total Eng Displ = $349.84\ in^3$

YOU CAN SEE THAT this engine's displacement is *approximately* **350 cubic inches**. This is the way the cubic inch displacement is estimated for some engine's that are produced!

CHAPTER 3

BORE - TO - STROKE RATIO

THE SIGNIFICANCE OF THIS factor is that it affects the rate or how fast the engine will rev. It is accomplished by the down force that is exerted on top of the piston by the burning air-fuel mixture during the power stroke.

THE LARGER THE CYLINDER bore(diameter) or cylinder area(see Figure 3-1), the greater will be the down force on top of the piston for a given compression ratio and air/fuel mixture.

THE STROKE'S(see Figure 3-2) influence arises from the fact that when its length is changed, the crankshaft's inertia(its resistance to turning) is also

Figure 3-1: The size of the cylinder bores shown will greatly affect the amount of force exerted on the piston during the engine's power phase. Photograph -- Courtesy of GM Performance Parts.

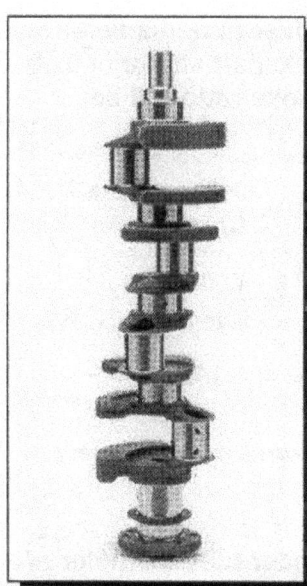

Figure 3-2: The crank throw is measured from the centerline of the crank's snout(top) to the centerline of any of the rod journals. *"The stroke is equal to two times the crank throw"!*

Photograph -- Courtesy of Crower Cams and Equipment Company.

changed, which is due somewhat in part to its total *mass*.

> **The larger the cylinder bore(diameter) or cylinder area, the greater will be the down force on top of the piston for a given compression ratio(and everything else being equal)...**

GENERALLY, THE LARGER THE ratio the better, this includes taking the engine's mechanical and physical limitations very much into consideration.

THE EQUATION FOR THE *cylinder bore -to- crankshaft stroke(bore -to- stroke ratio) ratio* is ...

$$\text{Bore -To- Stroke Ratio} = \frac{\text{Cylinder Bore}}{\text{Crank Stroke}}$$

EXAMPLE(3-1):
If an engine has a cylinder bore diameter of 4.00 inches, and a crankshaft stroke of 3.48 inches, its bore -to- stroke ratio will be...

$$\text{Bore -To- Stroke Ratio} = \frac{\text{Cylinder Bore}}{\text{Crank Stroke}}$$

$$\text{Bore -To- Stroke Ratio} = \frac{4.00 \text{ in}}{3.48 \text{ in}}$$

$$\text{Bore -To- Stroke Ratio} = 1.149$$

EXAMPLE(3-2):
If an engine has a cylinder bore diameter of 4.125 inches, and a crankshaft stroke of 3.48 inches, its bore -to- stroke ratio will be...

$$\text{Bore -To- Stroke Ratio} = \frac{\text{Cylinder Bore}}{\text{Crank Stroke}}$$

$$\text{Bore -To- Stroke Ratio} = \frac{4.125 \text{ in}}{3.48 \text{ in}}$$

$$\text{Bore -To- Stroke Ratio} = 1.1853$$

Close observation of these two examples shows that when the *cylinder bore diameter is increased* and the *crankshaft's stroke is held constant*, the engine's *bore -to- stroke ratio* <u>increases</u>. On the other hand, if the *cylinder bore diameter is held constant* and the *crankshaft's stroke is increased*, the engine's *bore -to- stroke ratio* <u>decreases</u>.

Also note that shortening the stroke will increase the engines rpm, up to a point, because the piston has a *shorter distance* to travel.

CHAPTER 4

ROD - TO - STROKE RATIO

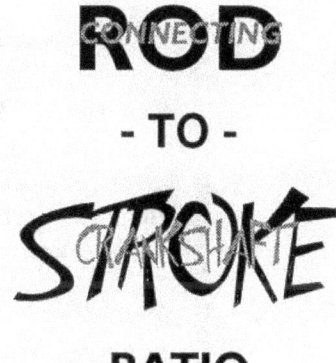

THE CONNECTING ROD'S length(Figure 4-1) has an effect upon the rate -- **piston travel per degree(^{o}) of crankshaft rotation** -- at which the piston will move away from top dead center(TDC) and from bottom dead center(BDC).

THE LONGER THE ROD IS IN RELATION TO THE stroke(the crankshaft stroke being constant), the slower the piston will move away from TDC on the intake and power strokes. The positive and negative aspects of this are:
1) There is more time to fill the cylinders at higher rpm's, and
2) There is a possible reduction in the intake manifold's vacuum at lower engine speeds -- depending on the type of induction system being used.

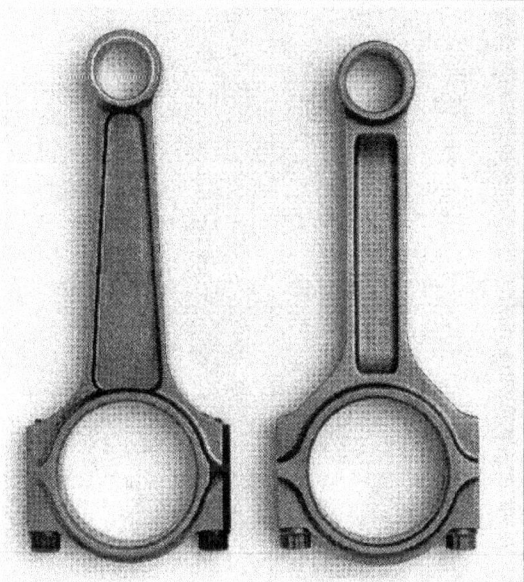

Figure 4-1: The longer rod(Left) can move a piston away from TDC slower than a shorter one(right); increasing the cylinder pressure. Photo -- Courtesy of Crower Cams and Equipment Company.

ON THE OTHER HAND A longer rod in relation to the stroke will move the piston away from BDC quicker and at a faster rate. This may give way to a possible reduction in time necessary to fill the cylinder, therefore, decreasing the amount of air-fuel mixture entering the cylinder during the earlier part of the compression stroke. Yet, this may be offset by an increase in scavenging of the exhaust gases during the exhaust process, if desired.

SINCE LARGER RATIOS TEND to increase cylinder pressures, this becomes very advantageous at higher engine speeds. Because, high cylinder pressures mean that there will be a greater down

...LARGER RATIOS TEND TO INCREASE CYLINDER PRESSURES...

force on top of the pistons, and a resulting increase in torque that is accompanied by an agnate boost in the engine's horsepower output.

IF THE CRANKSHAFT'S STROKE IS *increased* and the rod length is kept constant, the rod to stroke ratio will decrease. This will result in the piston be-

Figure 4-2: Increasing the stroke *(the distance from the centerline of the main journal to the centerline of the rod journal)* will lower the ratio if the rod length remains the same. Decreasing the stroke will increase the ratio if the rod length remains the same.
Photo -- Courtesy of Crower Cams and Equipment Company.

ing pulled away from TDC and BDC at a faster rate, therefore decreasing the pressure potential in the cylinder.

IF THE CRANKSHAFT'S STROKE IS *decreased* and the rod length is kept constant, the rod to stroke ratio will increase. This will result in the piston being pulled away from TDC and BDC at a slower rate, therefore increasing the pressure potential in the cylinder.

THE EQUATION FOR THE engine's rod to stroke ratio is:

$$\text{Rod -To- Stroke Ratio} = \frac{\text{Rod Length}}{\text{Crank Stroke}}$$

EXAMPLE(4-1):
If an engine has a rod length of 6.00 inches, and a crankshaft stroke of 3.48 inches, its rod -to- stroke ratio will be...

$$\text{Rod -To- Stroke Ratio} = \frac{\text{Rod Length}}{\text{Crank Stroke}}$$

$$\text{Rod -To- Stroke Ratio} = \frac{6.00 \text{ in}}{3.48 \text{ in}}$$

$$\text{Rod -To- Stroke Ratio} = 1.724$$

EXAMPLE(4-2):
If the engine's rod length of 6.00 inches were to remain constant, and if the crankshaft's stroke were decreased to 3.35 inches, the rod -to- stroke ratio will be...

$$\text{Rod -To- Stroke Ratio} = \frac{\text{Rod Length}}{\text{Crank Stroke}}$$

$$\text{Rod -To- Stroke Ratio} = \frac{6.00 \text{ in}}{3.35 \text{ in}}$$

$$\text{Rod -To- Stroke Ratio} = 1.791$$

IN SOME ENGINEERING APPLICATIONS THE R/L ratio is used instead of the above ratio(where, L is the crank throw). However, both ratios amount to the same thing.

CHAPTER 5

ROD ANGULARITY

THE CONNECTING ROD'S ANGULARITY IS the angle that the crankarm makes with the centerline of the cylinder bore when the connecting rod is at 90^0 to the crankarm(Figure 5-1). By engineering or increasing the rod angularity in one's engine, friction between the piston and cylinder wall will be reduced, and all side loading will be minimized between the pistons and cylinder walls, resulting in lower bearing loads and temperatures.

IN THE FOLLOWING EQUATION the rod angularity is denoted by the greek letter α(**alpha**).
Therefore,

α -- Rod Angularity
Crank Throw(r) = 1/2 x stroke
R -- Rod Length

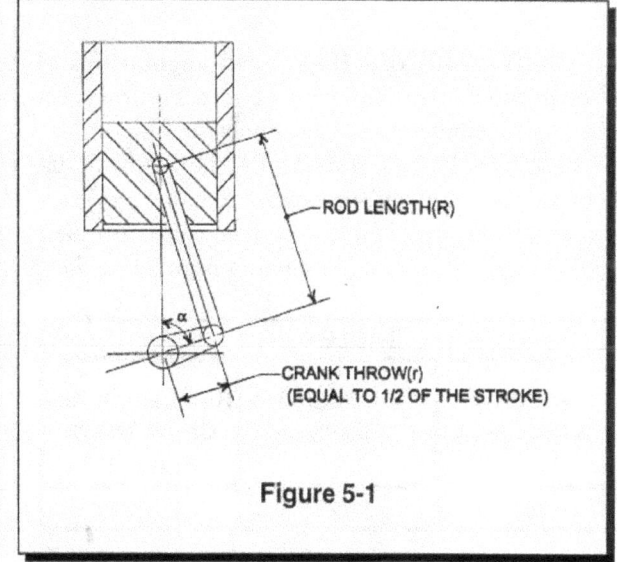

Figure 5-1

So,

$$\alpha = \text{Tan}^{-1}\left(\frac{\text{Rod Length}}{\text{Crank Throw}}\right)$$

Tan⁻¹ - IS CALLED the arctangent, or inverse tangent of the value in parentheses as shown above. This means, for example, to find that angle whose **tangent(R/r -or - Rod Length to Crank Throw ratio)** is **3.4483**. This value can be calculated using a *scientific calculator* possessing this function.

EXAMPLE(5-1a):
Now considering the previous given information from Chapter 4, Example(4-1) where,
R = 6.00", and S = Stroke = 3.48"...

This implies that,
Crank Throw = 1/2 x 3.48" = 1.74"

So,

$$\alpha = \text{Tan}^{-1}\left(\frac{\text{Rod Length}}{\text{Crank Throw}}\right)$$

$$\alpha = \text{Tan}^{-1}\left(\frac{6.00 \text{ in}}{1.74 \text{ in}}\right)$$

$$\alpha = \text{Tan}^{-1}(3.4483)$$

$$\alpha = 73.8278°$$

MANY ENGINES HAVE rod angularities of 70⁰ or greater. This can be used as a starting point in putting together your engine combination.

FOR YOUR INFORMATION, the following table of values are given for various rod angularities -- *in degrees and in radians* -- accompanied by their R/r(tangent) ratio, for angles ranging from **70⁰ to 77⁰**.

TABLE 5-1		
ANGLE(α) [in Degrees]	ANGLE(α) [in Radians]	Rod Length -to- Crank Throw Ratio(R/r)
70	1.2215	2.74748
70.1	1.22325	2.76247
70.2	1.22499	2.77761
70.3	1.22674	2.79289
70.4	1.22848	2.80833
70.5	1.23023	2.82391
70.6	1.23197	2.83965
70.7	1.23372	2.85555
70.8	1.23546	2.87161
70.9	1.23721	2.88783
71	1.23895	2.90421
71.1	1.2407	2.92076
71.2	1.24244	2.93748
71.3	1.24419	2.95437
71.4	1.24593	2.97144
71.5	1.24768	2.98868
71.6	1.24942	3.00611
71.7	1.25117	3.02372
71.8	1.25291	3.04152
71.9	1.25466	3.0595
72	1.2564	3.07768
72.1	1.25815	3.09606
72.2	1.25989	3.11464
72.3	1.26164	3.13341
72.4	1.26338	3.1524
72.5	1.26513	3.17159
72.6	1.26687	3.191
72.7	1.26862	3.21063
72.8	1.27036	3.23048
72.9	1.27211	3.25055
73	1.27385	3.27085
73.1	1.2756	3.29139
73.2	1.27734	3.31216
73.3	1.27909	3.33317
73.4	1.28083	3.35443
73.5	1.28258	3.37594
73.6	1.28432	3.39771

TABLE 5-1		
ANGLE(α) [in Degrees]	ANGLE(α) [in Radians]	Rod Length -to- Crank Throw Ratio(R/r)
73.7	1.28607	3.41973
73.8	1.28781	3.44202
73.9	1.28956	3.46458
74	1.2913	3.48741
74.1	1.29305	3.51053
74.2	1.29479	3.53393
74.3	1.29654	3.55761
74.4	1.29828	3.5816
74.5	1.30003	3.60588
74.6	1.30177	3.63048
74.7	1.30352	3.65538
74.8	1.30526	3.68061
74.9	1.30701	3.70616
75	1.30875	3.73205
75.1	1.3105	3.75828
75.2	1.31224	3.78485
75.3	1.31399	3.81177
75.4	1.31573	3.83906
75.5	1.31748	3.86671
75.6	1.31922	3.89474
75.7	1.32097	3.92316
75.8	1.32271	3.95196
75.9	1.32446	3.98117
76	1.3262	4.01078
76.1	1.32795	4.04081
76.2	1.32969	4.07127
76.3	1.33144	4.10216
76.4	1.33318	4.1335
76.5	1.33493	4.1653
76.6	1.33667	4.19756
76.7	1.33842	4.2303
76.8	1.34016	4.26352
76.9	1.34191	4.29724
77	1.34365	4.33148

EXAMPLE(5-1b):
For the "Rod Length -to- Crank Throw Ratio" value of 3.17159 chosen from Table 5-1, this indicates that the corresponding rod angularity would be 72.5°.
Which means that...

$$\alpha = \text{Tan}^{-1}\left(\frac{\text{Rod Length}}{\text{Crank Throw}}\right)$$

$\alpha = \text{Tan}^{-1}(3.17159)$

$\alpha = 72.5°$

TO CONVERT:

- "Degrees-to-radians", multiply the number of degrees times .01745(Degrees x .01745)

- "Radians-to-degrees", - divide the number of radians by .01745(Radians / .01745)

FIGURES 5.2 AND 5.3 ON THE FOLLOWING PAGE SHOW THE relationship between the **Rod Length -to- Crank Throw Ratio** versus the **Rod Angularity**, and the **Connecting Rod Length** versus the **Crankshaft Throw**, respectively, for a crankshaft throw of 1.74 inches.

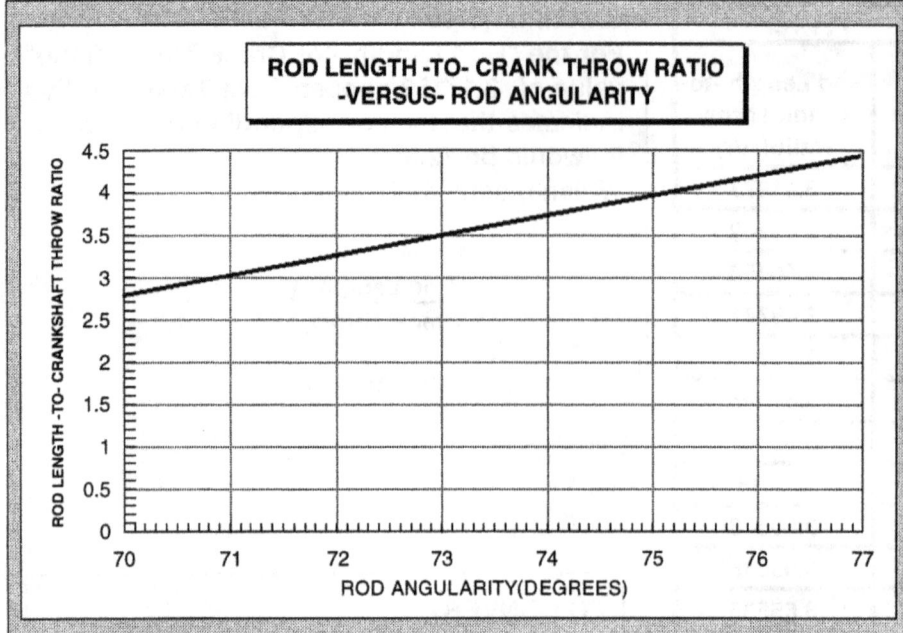

Figure 5-2: This graph is linear. If the engine's rod length -to- crank throw ratio is known, a horizontal line can be drawn to intersect the line of the graph at some point, it should be followed by drawing a vertical line through the same point to reveal the rod angularity. If the rod angularity is known, a vertical line can be drawn to intersect the line of the graph at some point, it should be followed by drawing a horizontal line through the same point to reveal the rod length -to- crank throw ratio.

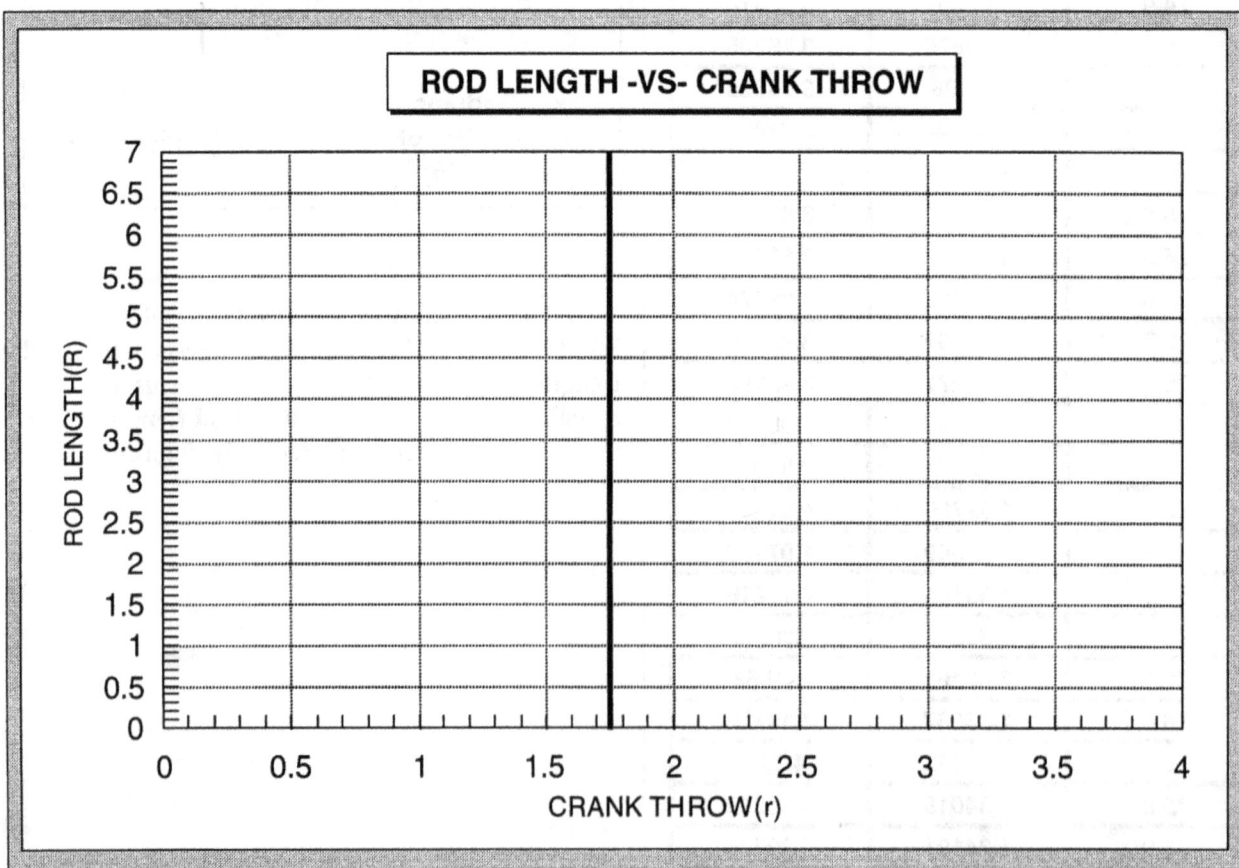

Figure 5-3: A graph of the 1.74 inch crank throw -- and any crank throw -- shows that it is vertical and independent of the rod length because the change in either the blocks deck height, deck height clearance volume, piston pin height could effect the rod length. However, in order for the rod angularity to be known, the rod length must be known for any crank throw.

CHAPTER 6

PISTON DISPLACEMENT

PISTON TRAVEL

PISTON DISPLACEMENT (PISTON TRAVEL) ARRIVES FROM the rotational motion of the crankshaft that is converted to rectilinear motion inside of the engine block's cylinder through the connecting rod(s).

THIS INCONSTANT DISPLACEMENT *(see Figure 6-1) can reveal some interesting features*. One

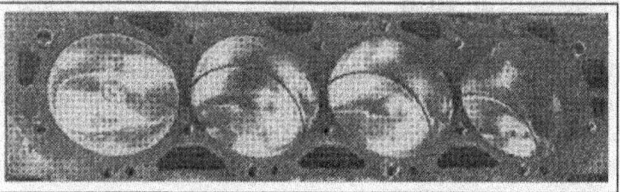

Figure 6-1: Each piston's displacement(travel) down from TDC -- as shown above -- is affected by the crank angle, crank throw, and rod length. Photograph -- Courtesy of GM Performance Parts

such feature is, the crank angle can be found once the *crank throw and rod length* are known*(see Table 5-1)*. This is very useful in selecting the proper valve timing. It can also be used to aid in the prevention of any valve-to-piston interference. This is very important in helping to avoid any possible premature engine failures due to assemblying errors.

THIS DISPLACEMENT IS mathematically defined as...

$$PD = \text{Crank Throw} \times \left[(1 - a) + \frac{\text{Crank Throw}}{2 \times \text{Rod length}} \times b\right]$$

Where,

- PD -- is the piston displacement calculated in inches(in)
- Crank Radius -- is the crank throw given in inches(in)
- Rod Length -- is the connecting rod length given in inches(in)
- a -- is the cos(pronounced -- cosine) of the crank angle(α) and is given in Table 6-1

- b -- is the sin(pronounced -- sine) of the crank angle(α) times itself[i.e. - sin(α) x sin(α)] and is given in Table 6-1

EXAMPLE(6a):
Using the data from Chapter - 5; where, the crank throw is equal to 1.74", the rod length is equal to 5.7"(such as in some small block Chevy engines...), and let the crank angle(α) be equal to 30^0(ATDC), the piston displacement will be...

For a crank angle(α) of 30^0(ATDC) from Table 6-1; <u>a</u> is equal to <u>0.866</u>, and <u>b</u> is equal to <u>0.25</u>.

$$PD = \text{Crank Throw} \times (1 - a + \frac{\text{Crank Throw}}{2 \times \text{Rod length}} \times b)$$

PD = 1.74 in x (1 - 0.866 + $\frac{1.74 \text{ in}}{2 \times 5.7 \text{ in}}$ x 0.25)

PD = 1.74 in x (1 - 0.866 + $\frac{1.74 \text{ in}}{11.4 \text{ in}}$ x 0.25)

PD = 1.74 in x (1 - 0.866 + 0.1526 x 0.25)

PD = 1.74 in x (1 - 0.866 + 0.0382)

PD = 1.74 in x (0.1722)

PD = 0.2996 in

NOW, FOR PURPOSES OF COMPARISON, two other values will be substituted into the piston displacement equation. These values are for crank angles of $\alpha = 60^0$ and $\alpha = 90^0$, respectively. Notice the results of these three displacements.

EXAMPLE(6b):
For a crank angle(α) of 60^0(ATDC) from Table 6-1; <u>a</u> is equal to <u>0.50</u>, and <u>b</u> is equal to <u>0.75</u>.

Therefore,

PD = 1.74 in x (1 - 0.50 + $\frac{1.74 \text{ in}}{2 \times 5.7 \text{ in}}$ x 0.75)

PD = 1.74 in x (1 - 0.50 + $\frac{1.74 \text{ in}}{11.4 \text{ in}}$ x 0.75)

PD = 1.74 in x (1 - 0.50 + 0.1526 x 0.75)

PD = 1.74 in x (1 - 0.50 + 0.1145)

PD = 1.74 in x (0.6145)

PD = 1.0692 in

EXAMPLE(6c):
For a crank angle(α) of 90^0(ATDC) from Table 6-1; <u>a</u> is equal to <u>0</u>, and <u>b</u> is equal to <u>1</u>.

Therefore,

PD = 1.74 in x (1 - 0 + $\frac{1.74 \text{ in}}{2 \times 5.7 \text{ in}}$ x 1)

PD = 1.74 in x (1 - 0 + $\frac{1.74 \text{ in}}{11.4 \text{ in}}$ x 1)

PD = 1.74 in x (1 - 0 + 0.1526 x 1)

PD = 1.74 in x (1 - 0 + 0.1526)

PD = 1.74 in x (1.1526)

PD = 2.0055 in

DID YOU NOTE ANY similarities or dissimilarities in these examples? If not, let's look at them together. An analysis of these three calculations reveals that at 30^0 ATDC(after top dead center) the piston has been displaced or traveled *only* .2996 inches or 8.61%[((.2996/3.48) x 100) = (.0861 x 100) = 8.61%] of the total travel(3.48 inch stroke).

At 60^0 and 90^0 -- two and three times the previous crank angle -- the piston travel is at 30.72% and 57.63% of the stroke. This should tell you that for any rod-to-stroke ratio, the piston travel will not necessarily be the same for each 30^0 increment of crankshaft rotation(Example: There is a 30^0 difference between 30^0 ATDC and 60^0 ATDC, and there is also a 30^0 difference between 60^0 ATDC and 90^0 ATDC). For this matter, this holds true for any other equal increments of crankshaft rotation. *See Table 6-2 for piston displacement values calculated from 0° to 360° based on both rod lengths of 5.7 and 6.0 inches, and a crank throw of 1.74 inches.*

NOW, THE NEXT THREE examples will be calculated using a **rod length of 6.00"**. Compare these examples to the three previous *Examples(6a, 6b, 6c)* and note the difference.

EXAMPLE(6d):
For a crank throw of 1.74 inches, a rod length of 6.00 inches, and a crank angle(α) of 30°(ATDC) from Table 6-1; <u>a</u> is equal to <u>0.866</u>, and <u>b</u> is equal to <u>0.25</u>.

Then,

$$PD = \text{Crank Throw} \times (1 - a + \frac{\text{Crank Throw}}{2 \times \text{Rod length}} \times b)$$

PD = 1.74 in x (1 - 0.866 + $\frac{1.74 \text{ in}}{2 \times 6.0 \text{ in}}$ x 0.25)

PD = 1.74 in x (1 - 0.866 + $\frac{1.74 \text{ in}}{12.0 \text{ in}}$ x 0.25)

PD = 1.74 in x (1 - 0.866 + 0.145 x 0.25)

PD = 1.74 in x (1 - 0.866 + 0.0363)

PD = 1.74 in x (0.1703)

PD = 0.2963 in

EXAMPLE(6e):
For a crank angle(α) of 60°(ATDC) from Table 6-1; <u>a</u> is equal to <u>0.50</u>, and <u>b</u> is equal to <u>0.75</u>.

Therefore,

PD = 1.74 in x (1 - 0.50 + $\frac{1.74 \text{ in}}{2 \times 6.0 \text{ in}}$ x 0.75)

PD = 1.74 in x (1 - 0.50 + $\frac{1.74 \text{ in}}{12.0 \text{ in}}$ x 0.75)

PD = 1.74 in x (1 - 0.50 + 0.145 x 0.75)

PD = 1.74 in x (1 - 0.50 + 0.1088)

PD = 1.74 in x (0.6088)

PD = 1.0593 in

EXAMPLE(6f):
For a crank angle(α) of 90°(ATDC) from Table 6-1; <u>a</u> is equal to <u>0</u>, and <u>b</u> is equal to <u>1</u>.

Hence,

PD = 1.74 in x (1 - 0 + $\frac{1.74 \text{ in}}{2 \times 6.0 \text{ in}}$ x 1)

PD = 1.74 in x (1 - 0 + $\frac{1.74 \text{ in}}{12.0 \text{ in}}$ x 1)

PD = 1.74 in x (1 - 0 + 0.145 x 1)

PD = 1.74 in x (1 - 0 + 0.145)

PD = 1.74 in x (1.145)

PD = 1.9923 in

THE RESULTS OF THESE calculations are also listed in Table 6-2, preceded by a graph of both sets of values shown in Figure 6-2. An extended number of degrees of crankshaft rotation were included in the table and graph. This was done to show the relationship between the crank angle and piston displacement after the completion of two strokes of the crankshaft (from TDC to BDC & from BDC to TDC).

BEAR IN MIND that the actual measurements of a piston's displacement may vary from the calculated values, due to bearing and piston pin clearances, the lubricant's film thickness, and, if the crankshaft needs straightening(is bent!!).

THE VALUES FOR THE TRIGONOMETRIC FUNCTIONS[**cos(α)** & **sin(α)**] can be calculated -- for <u>a</u> and <u>b</u> -- from zero degrees(0°) to three hundred and sixty degrees(360°) by utilizing a scientific calculator possessing these functions. They can otherwise be chosen from Table 6-2, shown hereafter.

TABLE 6-1		
CRANK ANGLE(α) [in Degrees]	a	b
0	1	0
1	0.9998	0.0003
2	0.9994	0.0012
3	0.9986	0.0027
4	0.9976	0.0049
5	0.9962	0.0076
6	0.9945	0.0109
7	0.9925	0.0149
8	0.9903	0.0194
9	0.9877	0.0245
10	0.9848	0.0302
11	0.9816	0.0364
12	0.9781	0.0432
13	0.9744	0.0506
14	0.9703	0.0585
15	0.9659	0.067
16	0.9613	0.076
17	0.9563	0.0855
18	0.9511	0.0955
19	0.9455	0.106
20	0.9397	0.117
21	0.9336	0.1284
22	0.9272	0.1403
23	0.9205	0.1527
24	0.9135	0.1654
25	0.9063	0.1786
26	0.8988	0.1922
27	0.891	0.2061
28	0.8829	0.2204
29	0.8746	0.235
30	0.866	0.25
31	0.8572	0.2653
32	0.848	0.2808
33	0.8387	0.2966
34	0.829	0.3127
35	0.8192	0.329
36	0.809	0.3455
37	0.7986	0.3622
38	0.788	0.379
39	0.7771	0.396
40	0.766	0.4132
41	0.7547	0.4304
42	0.7431	0.4477
43	0.7314	0.4651
44	0.7193	0.4826
45	0.7071	0.5
46	0.6947	0.5174
47	0.682	0.5349
48	0.6691	0.5523
49	0.6561	0.5696
50	0.6428	0.5868
51	0.6293	0.604
52	0.6157	0.621
53	0.6018	0.6378
54	0.5878	0.6545
55	0.5736	0.671
56	0.5592	0.6873
57	0.5446	0.7034
58	0.5299	0.7192
59	0.515	0.7347
60	0.5	0.75
61	0.4848	0.765
62	0.4695	0.7796
63	0.454	0.7939
64	0.4384	0.8078
65	0.4226	0.8214
66	0.4067	0.8346
67	0.3907	0.8473
68	0.3746	0.8597
69	0.3584	0.8716
70	0.342	0.883
71	0.3256	0.894

TABLE 6-1		
CRANK ANGLE(α) [in Degrees]	a	b
72	0.309	0.9045
73	0.2924	0.9145
74	0.2756	0.924
75	0.2588	0.933
76	0.2419	0.9415
77	0.225	0.9494
78	0.2079	0.9568
79	0.1908	0.9636
80	0.1736	0.9698
81	0.1564	0.9755
82	0.1392	0.9806
83	0.1219	0.9851
84	0.1045	0.9891
85	0.0872	0.9924
86	0.0698	0.9951
87	0.0523	0.9973
88	0.0349	0.9988
89	0.0175	0.9997
90	0	1
91	-0.0175	0.9997
92	-0.0349	0.9988
93	-0.0523	0.9973
94	-0.0698	0.9951
95	-0.0872	0.9924
96	-0.1045	0.9891
97	-0.1219	0.9851
98	-0.1392	0.9806
99	-0.1564	0.9755
100	-0.1736	0.9698
101	-0.1908	0.9636
102	-0.2079	0.9568
103	-0.225	0.9494
104	-0.2419	0.9415
105	-0.2588	0.933
106	-0.2756	0.924
107	-0.2924	0.9145

TABLE 6-1		
CRANK ANGLE(α) [in Degrees]	a	b
108	-0.309	0.9045
109	-0.3256	0.894
110	-0.342	0.883
111	-0.3584	0.8716
112	-0.3746	0.8597
113	-0.3907	0.8473
114	-0.4067	0.8346
115	-0.4226	0.8214
116	-0.4384	0.8078
117	-0.454	0.7939
118	-0.4695	0.7796
119	-0.4848	0.765
120	-0.5	0.75
121	-0.515	0.7347
122	-0.5299	0.7192
123	-0.5446	0.7034
124	-0.5592	0.6873
125	-0.5736	0.671
126	-0.5878	0.6545
127	-0.6018	0.6378
128	-0.6157	0.621
129	-0.6293	0.604
130	-0.6428	0.5868
131	-0.6561	0.5696
132	-0.6691	0.5523
133	-0.682	0.5349
134	-0.6947	0.5174
135	-0.7071	0.5
136	-0.7193	0.4826
137	-0.7314	0.4651
138	-0.7431	0.4477
139	-0.7547	0.4304
140	-0.766	0.4132
141	-0.7771	0.396
142	-0.788	0.379
143	-0.7986	0.3622

TABLE 6-1		
CRANK ANGLE(α) [in Degrees]	a	b
144	-0.809	0.3455
145	-0.8192	0.329
146	-0.829	0.3127
147	-0.8387	0.2966
148	-0.848	0.2808
149	-0.8572	0.2653
150	-0.866	0.25
151	-0.8746	0.235
152	-0.8829	0.2204
153	-0.891	0.2061
154	-0.8988	0.1922
155	-0.9063	0.1786
156	-0.9135	0.1654
157	-0.9205	0.1527
158	-0.9272	0.1403
159	-0.9336	0.1284
160	-0.9397	0.117
161	-0.9455	0.106
162	-0.9511	0.0955
163	-0.9563	0.0855
164	-0.9613	0.076
165	-0.9659	0.067
166	-0.9703	0.0585
167	-0.9744	0.0506
168	-0.9781	0.0432
169	-0.9816	0.0364
170	-0.9848	0.0302
171	-0.9877	0.0245
172	-0.9903	0.0194
173	-0.9925	0.0149
174	-0.9945	0.0109
175	-0.9962	0.0076
176	-0.9976	0.0049
177	-0.9986	0.0027
178	-0.9994	0.0012
179	-0.9998	0.0003
180	-1	0
181	-0.9998	0.0003
182	-0.9994	0.0012
183	-0.9986	0.0027
184	-0.9976	0.0049
185	-0.9962	0.0076
186	-0.9945	0.0109
187	-0.9925	0.0149
188	-0.9903	0.0194
189	-0.9877	0.0245
190	-0.9848	0.0302
191	-0.9816	0.0364
192	-0.9781	0.0432
193	-0.9744	0.0506
194	-0.9703	0.0585
195	-0.9659	0.067
196	-0.9613	0.076
197	-0.9563	0.0855
198	-0.9511	0.0955
199	-0.9455	0.106
200	-0.9397	0.117
201	-0.9336	0.1284
202	-0.9272	0.1403
203	-0.9205	0.1527
204	-0.9135	0.1654
205	-0.9063	0.1786
206	-0.8988	0.1922
207	-0.891	0.2061
208	-0.8829	0.2204
209	-0.8746	0.235
210	-0.866	0.25
211	-0.8572	0.2653
212	-0.848	0.2808
213	-0.8387	0.2966
214	-0.829	0.3127
215	-0.8192	0.329

TABLE 6-1		
CRANK ANGLE(α) [in Degrees]	a	b
216	-0.809	0.3455
217	-0.7986	0.3622
218	-0.788	0.379
219	-0.7771	0.396
220	-0.766	0.4132
221	-0.7547	0.4304
222	-0.7431	0.4477
223	-0.7314	0.4651
224	-0.7193	0.4826
225	-0.7071	0.5
226	-0.6947	0.5174
227	-0.682	0.5349
228	-0.6691	0.5523
229	-0.6561	0.5696
230	-0.6428	0.5868
231	-0.6293	0.604
232	-0.6157	0.621
233	-0.6018	0.6378
234	-0.5878	0.6545
235	-0.5736	0.671
236	-0.5592	0.6873
237	-0.5446	0.7034
238	-0.5299	0.7192
239	-0.515	0.7347
240	-0.5	0.75
241	-0.4848	0.765
242	-0.4695	0.7796
243	-0.454	0.7939
244	-0.4384	0.8078
245	-0.4226	0.8214
246	-0.4067	0.8346
247	-0.3907	0.8473
248	-0.3746	0.8597
249	-0.3584	0.8716
250	-0.342	0.883
251	-0.3256	0.894
252	-0.309	0.9045
253	-0.2924	0.9145
254	-0.2756	0.924
255	-0.2588	0.933
256	-0.2419	0.9415
257	-0.225	0.9494
258	-0.2079	0.9568
259	-0.1908	0.9636
260	-0.1736	0.9698
261	-0.1564	0.9755
262	-0.1392	0.9806
263	-0.1219	0.9851
264	-0.1045	0.9891
265	-0.0872	0.9924
266	-0.0698	0.9951
267	-0.0523	0.9973
268	-0.0349	0.9988
269	-0.0175	0.9997
270	0	1
271	0.0175	0.9997
272	0.0349	0.9988
273	0.0523	0.9973
274	0.0698	0.9951
275	0.0872	0.9924
276	0.1045	0.9891
277	0.1219	0.9851
278	0.1392	0.9806
279	0.1564	0.9755
280	0.1736	0.9698
281	0.1908	0.9636
282	0.2079	0.9568
283	0.225	0.9494
284	0.2419	0.9415
285	0.2588	0.933
286	0.2756	0.924
287	0.2924	0.9145

TABLE 6-1

CRANK ANGLE(α) [in Degrees]	a	b	CRANK ANGLE(α) [in Degrees]	a	b
288	0.309	0.9045	324	0.809	0.3455
289	0.3256	0.894	325	0.8192	0.329
290	0.342	0.883	326	0.829	0.3127
291	0.3584	0.8716	327	0.8387	0.2966
292	0.3746	0.8597	328	0.848	0.2808
293	0.3907	0.8473	329	0.8572	0.2653
294	0.4067	0.8346	330	0.866	0.25
295	0.4226	0.8214	331	0.8746	0.235
296	0.4384	0.8078	332	0.8829	0.2204
297	0.454	0.7939	333	0.891	0.2061
298	0.4695	0.7796	334	0.8988	0.1922
299	0.4848	0.765	335	0.9063	0.1786
300	0.5	0.75	336	0.9135	0.1654
301	0.515	0.7347	337	0.9205	0.1527
302	0.5299	0.7192	338	0.9272	0.1403
303	0.5446	0.7034	339	0.9336	0.1284
304	0.5592	0.6873	340	0.9397	0.117
305	0.5736	0.671	341	0.9455	0.106
306	0.5878	0.6545	342	0.9511	0.0955
307	0.6018	0.6378	343	0.9563	0.0855
308	0.6157	0.621	344	0.9613	0.076
309	0.6293	0.604	345	0.9659	0.067
310	0.6428	0.5868	346	0.9703	0.0585
311	0.6561	0.5696	347	0.9744	0.0506
312	0.6691	0.5523	348	0.9781	0.0432
313	0.682	0.5349	349	0.9816	0.0364
314	0.6947	0.5174	350	0.9848	0.0302
315	0.7071	0.5	351	0.9877	0.0245
316	0.7193	0.4826	352	0.9903	0.0194
317	0.7314	0.4651	353	0.9925	0.0149
318	0.7431	0.4477	354	0.9945	0.0109
319	0.7547	0.4304	355	0.9962	0.0076
320	0.766	0.4132	356	0.9976	0.0049
321	0.7771	0.396	357	0.9986	0.0027
322	0.788	0.379	358	0.9994	0.0012
323	0.7986	0.3622	359	0.9998	0.0003

TABLE 6-1		
CRANK ANGLE(α) [in Degrees]	a	b
360	1	0

A GRAPH OF THE crank angle(α) versus both rod lengths of 5.7 inch and 6.0 inches is shown in Figure 6-2 for a crank throw of 1.74 inches. After the crankshaft rotates past 180^0 from TDC, note that the piston displacement begins to decrease as the piston ascends on the compression stroke or exhaust stroke. This is less than a full stroke of the crankshaft which is 3.48 inches. The piston displacement is equal to the crankshaft's stroke at 180^0 of crankshaft rotation from top dead center to bottom dead center during the intake or power stroke. It is also equal to the crankshaft's stroke when the crankshaft rotates from BDC through 180^0 of crankshaft rotation(or until it rotates to the TDC position). Remember the crank throw is equal to one-half(1/2) the stroke(Example: 3.48"/2 = 1.74"), or the stroke is equal to two(2) times the crank throw(Example: 2 x 1.74" = 3.48").

TABLE 6-2 THAT FOLLOWS THE GRAPH SHOWS THE CHANGES IN piston displacement for both rod lengths. Close observation of the graph shows that both graphs almost coincide. This is the reason why the curve of both graphs look like one line. However, an analyses of the data in Table 6-2 reveals the minor changes in displacement for each degree of crankshaft rotation for each rod length.

[Check out the extra examples added at the end of this chapter!]

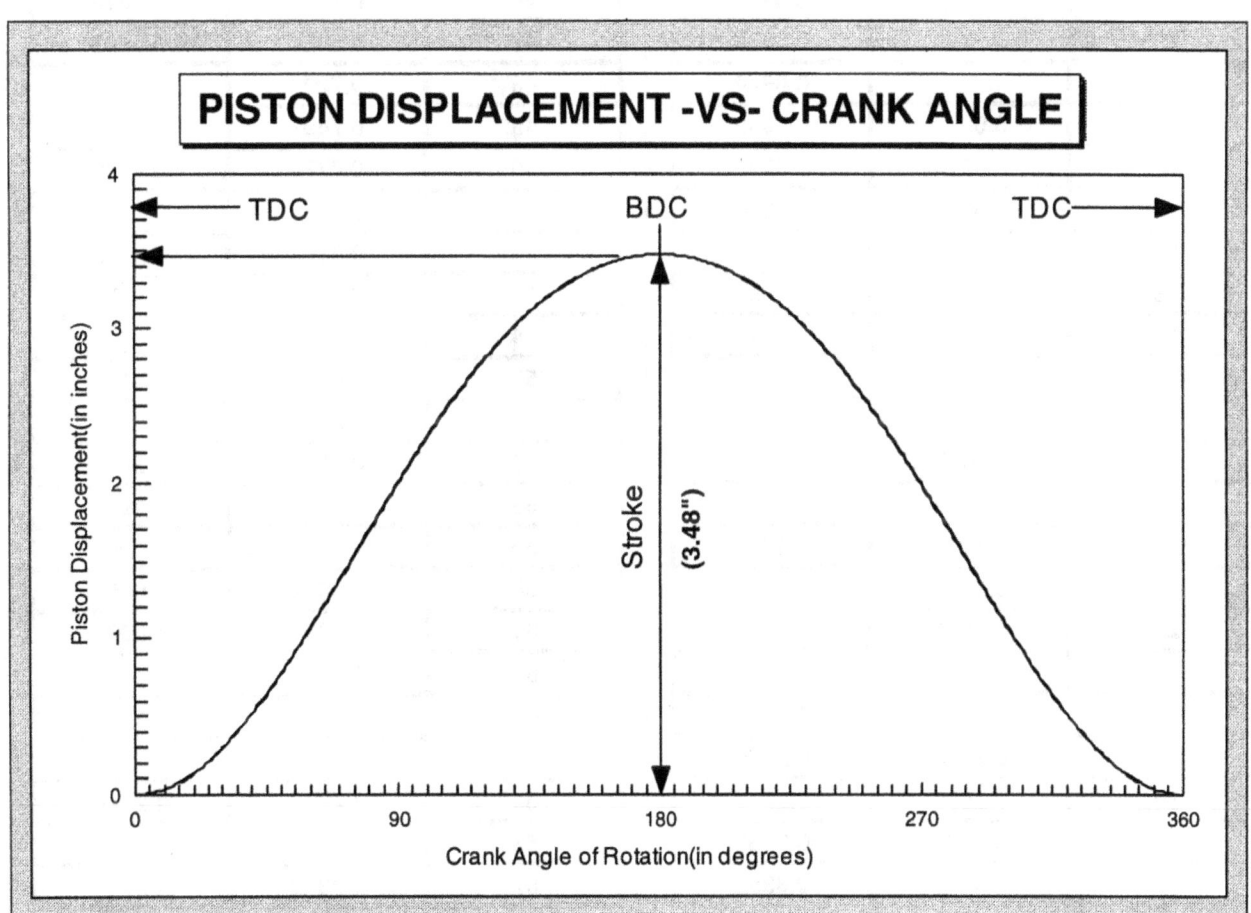

Figure 6-2: The lines' irregularity shows that both graphs almost coincide. The piston's displacement(travel) of both graphs increases from 0^0(TDC) to 180^0(BDC), and it is equal to the stroke at BDC. The piston displacement decreases from 180^0(BDC) to 360^0(TDC) as the piston ascends toward TDC.

TABLE 6-2

CRANK ANGLE(α) [in Degrees]	Piston Travel (For a 5.7" Rod Length & 1.74" Crank Throw)	Piston Travel (For a 6.0" Rod Length & 1.74" Crank Throw)
0	0	0
1	0.0003	0.0003
2	0.0014	0.0014
3	0.0031	0.0031
4	0.0055	0.0055
5	0.0086	0.0085
6	0.0124	0.0123
7	0.0169	0.0167
8	0.0221	0.0218
9	0.0279	0.0276
10	0.0344	0.034
11	0.0416	0.0412
12	0.0495	0.0489
13	0.058	0.0574
14	0.0672	0.0665
15	0.0771	0.0762
16	0.0876	0.0866
17	0.0987	0.0976
18	0.1105	0.1093
19	0.1229	0.1215
20	0.136	0.1344
21	0.1497	0.148
22	0.164	0.1621
23	0.1789	0.1768
24	0.1944	0.1922
25	0.2105	0.2081
26	0.2271	0.2246
27	0.2444	0.2416
28	0.2622	0.2593
29	0.2806	0.2775
30	0.2995	0.2962
31	0.319	0.3155
32	0.339	0.3352
33	0.3595	0.3556
34	0.3805	0.3764
35	0.402	0.3977
36	0.4241	0.4195
37	0.4466	0.4418
38	0.4695	0.4645
39	0.4929	0.4877
40	0.5168	0.5113
41	0.5411	0.5354
42	0.5658	0.5599
43	0.591	0.5848
44	0.6165	0.6101
45	0.6424	0.6358
46	0.6687	0.6618
47	0.6954	0.6883
48	0.7224	0.715
49	0.7497	0.7422
50	0.7774	0.7696
51	0.8054	0.7974
52	0.8337	0.8254
53	0.8622	0.8538
54	0.8911	0.8824
55	0.9202	0.9113
56	0.9495	0.9404
57	0.9791	0.9698
58	1.0089	0.9994
59	1.039	1.0292
60	1.0692	1.0592
61	1.0996	1.0894
62	1.1302	1.1198
63	1.1609	1.1504
64	1.1918	1.181
65	1.2228	1.2119
66	1.2539	1.2428
67	1.2852	1.2739
68	1.3165	1.3051
69	1.3479	1.3363

TABLE 6-2

CRANK ANGLE(α) [in Degrees]	Piston Travel (For a 5.7" Rod Length & 1.74" Crank Throw)	Piston Travel (For a 6.0" Rod Length & 1.74" Crank Throw)	CRANK ANGLE(α) [in Degrees]	Piston Travel (For a 5.7" Rod Length & 1.74" Crank Throw)	Piston Travel (For a 6.0" Rod Length & 1.74" Crank Throw)
70	1.3794	1.3677	105	2.4381	2.4257
71	1.4109	1.3991	106	2.465	2.4527
72	1.4425	1.4305	107	2.4916	2.4795
73	1.4742	1.462	108	2.5179	2.5059
74	1.5058	1.4935	109	2.5439	2.532
75	1.5374	1.5251	110	2.5696	2.5579
76	1.5691	1.5566	111	2.595	2.5835
77	1.6007	1.5881	112	2.6201	2.6087
78	1.6323	1.6196	113	2.6449	2.6337
79	1.6639	1.6511	114	2.6694	2.6583
80	1.6954	1.6825	115	2.6935	2.6826
81	1.7269	1.7139	116	2.7173	2.7066
82	1.7583	1.7453	117	2.7408	2.7302
83	1.7896	1.7765	118	2.7639	2.7536
84	1.8208	1.8077	119	2.7867	2.7766
85	1.8519	1.8387	120	2.8092	2.7992
86	1.8829	1.8697	121	2.8313	2.8215
87	1.9138	1.9005	122	2.8531	2.8435
88	1.9445	1.9313	123	2.8745	2.8651
89	1.9751	1.9619	124	2.8955	2.8864
90	2.0056	1.9923	125	2.9162	2.9073
91	2.0359	2.0226	126	2.9366	2.9279
92	2.066	2.0527	127	2.9565	2.9481
93	2.0959	2.0827	128	2.9762	2.9679
94	2.1257	2.1124	129	2.9954	2.9874
95	2.1552	2.142	130	3.0143	3.0065
96	2.1846	2.1714	131	3.0328	3.0252
97	2.2137	2.2006	132	3.051	3.0436
98	2.2426	2.2296	133	3.0687	3.0616
99	2.2713	2.2583	134	3.0861	3.0793
100	2.2997	2.2868	135	3.1032	3.0965
101	2.3279	2.3151	136	3.1198	3.1134
102	2.3559	2.3432	137	3.1361	3.1299
103	2.3836	2.3709	138	3.152	3.146
104	2.411	2.3985	139	3.1675	3.1618

TABLE 6-2

CRANK ANGLE(α) [in Degrees]	Piston Travel (For a 5.7" Rod Length & 1.74" Crank Throw)	Piston Travel (For a 6.0" Rod Length & 1.74" Crank Throw)
140	3.1826	3.1772
141	3.1974	3.1922
142	3.2118	3.2068
143	3.2258	3.221
144	3.2394	3.2349
145	3.2527	3.2483
146	3.2656	3.2614
147	3.2781	3.2741
148	3.2902	3.2865
149	3.3019	3.2984
150	3.3133	3.31
151	3.3243	3.3211
152	3.3349	3.3319
153	3.3451	3.3424
154	3.3549	3.3524
155	3.3644	3.362
156	3.3735	3.3713
157	3.3822	3.3802
158	3.3906	3.3887
159	3.3985	3.3968
160	3.4061	3.4046
161	3.4134	3.4119
162	3.4202	3.4189
163	3.4267	3.4255
164	3.4328	3.4318
165	3.4385	3.4376
166	3.4439	3.4431
167	3.4488	3.4482
168	3.4535	3.4529
169	3.4577	3.4572
170	3.4616	3.4612
171	3.4651	3.4648
172	3.4682	3.468
173	3.471	3.4708
174	3.4734	3.4732
175	3.4754	3.4753
176	3.4771	3.477
177	3.4783	3.4783
178	3.4793	3.4792
179	3.4798	3.4798
180	3.48	3.48
181	3.4798	3.4798
182	3.4793	3.4792
183	3.4783	3.4783
184	3.4771	3.477
185	3.4754	3.4753
186	3.4734	3.4732
187	3.471	3.4708
188	3.4682	3.468
189	3.4651	3.4648
190	3.4616	3.4612
191	3.4577	3.4572
192	3.4535	3.4529
193	3.4488	3.4482
194	3.4439	3.4431
195	3.4385	3.4376
196	3.4328	3.4318
197	3.4267	3.4255
198	3.4202	3.4189
199	3.4134	3.4119
200	3.4061	3.4046
201	3.3985	3.3968
202	3.3906	3.3887
203	3.3822	3.3802
204	3.3735	3.3713
205	3.3644	3.362
206	3.3549	3.3524
207	3.3451	3.3424
208	3.3349	3.3319
209	3.3243	3.3211

TABLE 6-2		
CRANK ANGLE(α) [in Degrees]	Piston Travel (For a 5.7" Rod Length & 1.74" Crank Throw)	Piston Travel (For a 6.0" Rod Length & 1.74" Crank Throw)
210	3.3133	3.31
211	3.3019	3.2984
212	3.2902	3.2865
213	3.2781	3.2741
214	3.2656	3.2614
215	3.2527	3.2483
216	3.2394	3.2349
217	3.2258	3.221
218	3.2118	3.2068
219	3.1974	3.1922
220	3.1826	3.1772
221	3.1675	3.1618
222	3.152	3.146
223	3.1361	3.1299
224	3.1198	3.1134
225	3.1032	3.0965
226	3.0861	3.0793
227	3.0687	3.0616
228	3.051	3.0436
229	3.0328	3.0252
230	3.0143	3.0065
231	2.9954	2.9874
232	2.9762	2.9679
233	2.9565	2.9481
234	2.9366	2.9279
235	2.9162	2.9073
236	2.8955	2.8864
237	2.8745	2.8651
238	2.8531	2.8435
239	2.8313	2.8215
240	2.8092	2.7992
241	2.7867	2.7766
242	2.7639	2.7536
243	2.7408	2.7302
244	2.7173	2.7066
245	2.6935	2.6826
246	2.6694	2.6583
247	2.6449	2.6337
248	2.6201	2.6087
249	2.595	2.5835
250	2.5696	2.5579
251	2.5439	2.532
252	2.5179	2.5059
253	2.4916	2.4795
254	2.465	2.4527
255	2.4381	2.4257
256	2.411	2.3985
257	2.3836	2.3709
258	2.3559	2.3432
259	2.3279	2.3151
260	2.2997	2.2868
261	2.2713	2.2583
262	2.2426	2.2296
263	2.2137	2.2006
264	2.1846	2.1714
265	2.1552	2.142
266	2.1257	2.1124
267	2.0959	2.0827
268	2.066	2.0527
269	2.0359	2.0226
270	2.0056	1.9923
271	1.9751	1.9619
272	1.9445	1.9313
273	1.9138	1.9005
274	1.8829	1.8697
275	1.8519	1.8387
276	1.8208	1.8077
277	1.7896	1.7765
278	1.7583	1.7453
279	1.7269	1.7139

TABLE 6-2

CRANK ANGLE(α) [in Degrees]	Piston Travel (For a 5.7" Rod Length & 1.74" Crank Throw)	Piston Travel (For a 6.0" Rod Length & 1.74" Crank Throw)
280	1.6954	1.6825
281	1.6639	1.6511
282	1.6323	1.6196
283	1.6007	1.5881
284	1.5691	1.5566
285	1.5374	1.5251
286	1.5058	1.4935
287	1.4742	1.462
288	1.4425	1.4305
289	1.4109	1.3991
290	1.3794	1.3677
291	1.3479	1.3363
292	1.3165	1.3051
293	1.2852	1.2739
294	1.2539	1.2428
295	1.2228	1.2119
296	1.1918	1.181
297	1.1609	1.1504
298	1.1302	1.1198
299	1.0996	1.0894
300	1.0692	1.0592
301	1.039	1.0292
302	1.0089	0.9994
303	0.9791	0.9698
304	0.9495	0.9404
305	0.9202	0.9113
306	0.8911	0.8824
307	0.8622	0.8538
308	0.8337	0.8254
309	0.8054	0.7974
310	0.7774	0.7696
311	0.7497	0.7422
312	0.7224	0.715
313	0.6954	0.6883
314	0.6687	0.6618
315	0.6424	0.6358
316	0.6165	0.6101
317	0.591	0.5848
318	0.5658	0.5599
319	0.5411	0.5354
320	0.5168	0.5113
321	0.4929	0.4877
322	0.4695	0.4645
323	0.4466	0.4418
324	0.4241	0.4195
325	0.402	0.3977
326	0.3805	0.3764
327	0.3595	0.3556
328	0.339	0.3352
329	0.319	0.3155
330	0.2995	0.2962
331	0.2806	0.2775
332	0.2622	0.2593
333	0.2444	0.2416
334	0.2271	0.2246
335	0.2105	0.2081
336	0.1944	0.1922
337	0.1789	0.1768
338	0.164	0.1621
339	0.1497	0.148
340	0.136	0.1344
341	0.1229	0.1215
342	0.1105	0.1093
343	0.0987	0.0976
344	0.0876	0.0866
345	0.0771	0.0762
346	0.0672	0.0665
347	0.058	0.0574
348	0.0495	0.0489
349	0.0416	0.0412

TABLE 6-2		
CRANK ANGLE(α) [in Degrees]	Piston Travel (For a 5.7" Rod Length & 1.74" Crank Throw)	Piston Travel (For a 6.0" Rod Length & 1.74" Crank Throw)
350	0.0344	0.034
351	0.0279	0.0276
352	0.0221	0.0218
353	0.0169	0.0167
354	0.0124	0.0123
355	0.0086	0.0085
356	0.0055	0.0055
357	0.0031	0.0031
358	0.0014	0.0014
359	0.0003	0.0003
360	0	0

THE FOLLOWING EXAMPLE WAS added in order to show how to calculate the piston displacement using a negative(-) value for $\underline{a}$, and to show the maximum piston displacement at a crank angle of 180^0.

EXAMPLE(6g):
For a crank angle of 180^0(BDC), a crank throw of 1.74", and rod length equal to 5.7", the piston displacement will be...

For a crank angle(α) of 180^0(BDC) from Table 6-1; $\underline{a}$ is equal to $\underline{-1}$, and $\underline{b}$ is equal to $\underline{0}$.

$$PD = \text{Crank Throw} \times [(1 - a) + \frac{\text{Crank Throw}}{2 \times \text{Rod length}} \times b]$$

$$PD = 1.74 \text{ in} \times (1 - (-1) + \frac{1.74 \text{ in}}{2 \times 5.7 \text{ in}} \times 0)$$

$$PD = 1.74 \text{ in} \times (1 + 1 + \frac{1.74 \text{ in}}{11.4 \text{ in}} \times 0)$$

$$PD = 1.74 \text{ in} \times (2 + 0.1526 \times 0)$$

$$PD = 1.74 \text{ in} \times (2 + 0)$$

$$PD = 1.74 \text{ in} \times 2$$

$$PD = 3.48 \text{ in}$$

THE NEXT EXAMPLE SHOWS THAT the piston displacement is equal to **zero(0)** for a crank angle of 360^0(*one revolution of the crankshaft*), because the piston has returned back to top dead center.

EXAMPLE(6h):
For a crank angle of 360^0(TDC), a crank throw of 1.74", and rod length equal to 5.7", the piston displacement will be...

For a crank angle(α) of 360^0(TDC) from Table 6-1; $\underline{a}$ is equal to $\underline{1}$, and $\underline{b}$ is equal to $\underline{0}$.

$$PD = 1.74 \text{ in} \times (1 - 1 + \frac{1.74 \text{ in}}{2 \times 5.7 \text{ in}} \times 0)$$

$$PD = 1.74 \text{ in} \times (0 + \frac{1.74 \text{ in}}{11.4 \text{ in}} \times 0)$$

$$PD = 1.74 \text{ in} \times (0 + 0.1526 \times 0)$$

$$PD = 1.74 \text{ in} \times (0 + 0)$$

$$PD = 1.74 \text{ in} \times 0$$

$$PD = 0 \text{ inches}$$

THE PISTON DISPLACEMENT SHOULD BE **zero(0)** at $\alpha=0^0$(TDC) & $\alpha=360^0$(TDC) of crankshaft rotation for any combination of crank throw and rod length.

IN SOME EXAMPLES THERE ARE some slight variations between the manually calculated values and the values given in Table 6-2. The reason for this difference is that the values in Table 6-2 were computer generated.

CALCULATIONS

CHAPTER 7

CYLINDER VOLUME
- VERSUS -
CRANK ANGLE

THE PRECEDING CHAPTERS in this book have focused on the engine's cubic inch displacement and piston displacement.

NONETHELESS, this chapter will concentrate on calculating the change in cylinder volume(swept volume) based on the crankshaft's rotation through a predetermined, or finite number of degrees. By knowing the area of the cylinder and the piston's displacement or the piston travel for a specified crank angle, the cylinder volume as a function of this crank angle can be computed(*see Figure 7-1, Figure 7-2 & Table 7-1*).

SOME MAJOR ADVANTAGES this constituent has to offer are: first, a better insight into choosing the proper valve timing(camshaft) for the engine, and second, adequate valve sizes for proper air-fuel flow into the engine. This is while taking the engine's optimum speed, vehicle weight, etc., into consideration for one's vehicle application.

THE EQUATION for calculating this cylinder volume is as follows:

Figure 7-1: The cylinder volume, that is the volume above the piston, is greater if the piston is located further down from the top(TDC location) of an engine's cylinder bore as shown above.
Photograph -- Courtesy of GM Performance Parts

Cylinder Volume = Cylinder Area x PD

Where,

Cylinder Volume -- is the volume of the cylinder corresponding to a desired crank angle, calculated in cubic inches(in^3)

Cylinder Area -- is the area of the cylinder calculated in square inches(in^2)

PD -- is the piston displacement calculated in inches(in)

EXAMPLE(7a):
Using the cylinder area of 12.56636 in² from EXAMPLE(2a), and a crank throw equal to 1.74", a rod length equal to 5.7"(such as in some small block Chevy engines...), and let the crank angle(α) be equal to 0°(TDC); the piston displacement will be...

For a crank angle(α) of 0°(TDC) from Table 6-1; **a** is equal to **1**, and **b** is equal to **0**.

$$PD = \text{Crank Throw} \times \left(1 - a + \frac{\text{Crank Throw}}{2 \times \text{Rod length}} \times b\right)$$

PD = 1.74 in × (1 - 1 + $\frac{1.74 \text{ in}}{2 \times 5.7 \text{ in}}$ × 0)

PD = 1.74 in × (0 + $\frac{1.74 \text{ in}}{11.4 \text{ in}}$ × 0)

PD = 1.74 in × (0 + 0.1526 × 0)

PD = 1.74 in × (0 + 0)

PD = 1.74 in × 0

PD = 0 inches

Since,

Cylinder Area = 12.56636 in²

Then,

$$\text{Cylinder Volume} = \text{Cylinder Area} \times \text{PD}$$

Cylinder Volume = 12.56636 in² × 0 inches

Cylinder Volume = 0 in³ (cu in)

EXAMPLE(7b):
Using the same data as in EXAMPLE(7a), and let the crank angle(α) be equal to 30°(ATDC); the piston displacement will be...

For a crank angle(α) of 30°(ATDC) from Table 6-1; **a** is equal to **0.866**, and **b** is equal to **0.25**.

Therefore,

PD = 1.74 in × (1 - 0.866 + $\frac{1.74 \text{ in}}{2 \times 5.7 \text{ in}}$ × 0.25)

PD = 1.74 in × (1 - 0.866 + $\frac{1.74 \text{ in}}{11.4 \text{ in}}$ × 0.25)

PD = 1.74 in × (1 - 0.866 + 0.1526 × 0.25)

PD = 1.74 in × (1 - 0.866 + 0.0382)

PD = 1.74 in × (0.1722)

PD = 0.2996 in

And,

Cylinder Area = 12.56636 in²

Therefore,

Cylinder Volume = 12.56636 in² × 0.2996 in

Cylinder Volume = 3.7649 in³ (cu in)

EXAMPLE(7c):
Using the same data as in EXAMPLE(7a), and let the crank angle(α) be equal to 60°(ATDC); the piston displacement will be...

For a crank angle(α) of 60°(ATDC) from Table 6-1; **a** is equal to **0.5**, and **b** is equal to **0.75**.

PD = 1.74 in × (1 - 0.50 + $\frac{1.74 \text{ in}}{2 \times 5.7 \text{ in}}$ × 0.75)

PD = 1.74 in × (1 - 0.50 + $\frac{1.74 \text{ in}}{11.4 \text{ in}}$ × 0.75)

PD = 1.74 in × (1 - 0.50 + 0.1526 × 0.75)

PD = 1.74 in × (1 - 0.50 + 0.1145)

PD = 1.74 in × (0.6145)

PD = 1.0692 in

And,

Cylinder Area = 12.56636 in²

Therefore,

Cylinder Volume = 12.56636 in² x 1.0692 in

Cylinder Volume = 13.436 in³ (cu in)

EXAMPLE(7d):
Using the same data as in EXAMPLE(7a), and let the crank angle(α) be equal to 90°(ATDC); the piston displacement will be...

For a crank angle(α) of 90°(ATDC) from Table 6-1; $\underline{a}$ is equal to $\underline{0}$, and $\underline{b}$ is equal to $\underline{1}$.

PD = 1.74 in x (1 - 0 + $\dfrac{1.74 \text{ in}}{2 \times 5.7 \text{ in}}$ x 1)

PD = 1.74 in x (1 - 0 + $\dfrac{1.74 \text{ in}}{11.4 \text{ in}}$ x 1)

PD = 1.74 in x (1 - 0 + 0.1526 x 1)

PD = 1.74 in x (1 - 0 + 0.1526)

PD = 1.74 in x (1.1526)

PD = 2.0055 in

And,

Cylinder Area = 12.56636 in²

Therefore,

Cylinder Volume = 12.56636 in² x 2.0055 in

Cylinder Volume = 25.2018 in³ (cu in)

EXAMPLE(7e):
Using the same data as in EXAMPLE(7a), and let the crank angle(α) be equal to 120°(ATDC); the piston displacement will be...

For a crank angle(α) of 120°(ATDC) from Table 6-1; $\underline{a}$ is equal to $\underline{-0.5}$, and $\underline{b}$ is equal to $\underline{0.75}$.

PD = 1.74 in x (1 - (-0.50) + $\dfrac{1.74 \text{ in}}{2 \times 5.7 \text{ in}}$ x 0.75)

PD = 1.74 in x (1 + 0.50 + $\dfrac{1.74 \text{ in}}{11.4 \text{ in}}$ x 0.75)

PD = 1.74 in x (1.50 + 0.1526 x 0.75)

PD = 1.74 in x (1.50 + 0.1145)

PD = 1.74 in x (1.6145)

PD = 2.8092 in

And,

Cylinder Area = 12.56636 in²

Therefore,

Cylinder Volume = 12.56636 in² x 2.8092 in

Cylinder Volume = 35.3014 in³ (cu in)

EXAMPLE(7f):
Using the same data as in EXAMPLE(7a), and let the crank angle(α) be equal to 150°(ATDC); the piston displacement will be...

For a crank angle(α) of 150°(ATDC) from Table 6-1; $\underline{a}$ is equal to $\underline{-0.866}$, and $\underline{b}$ is equal to $\underline{.25}$.

PD = 1.74 in x (1 - (-0.866) + $\dfrac{1.74 \text{ in}}{2 \times 5.7 \text{ in}}$ x 0.25)

PD = 1.74 in x (1 + 0.866 + $\dfrac{1.74 \text{ in}}{11.4 \text{ in}}$ x 0.25)

PD = 1.74 in x (1.866 + 0.1526 x 0.25)

PD = 1.74 in x (1.866 + 0.0382)

PD = 1.74 in x (1.9042)

PD = 3.3133 in

And,

Cylinder Area = 12.56636 in²

Therefore,

Cylinder Volume = 12.56636 in² x 3.3133 in

Cylinder Volume = 41.6361 in³ (cu in)

EXAMPLE(7g):
Using the same data as in EXAMPLE(7a), and let the crank angle(α) be equal to 180°(BDC); the piston displacement will be...

For a crank angle(α) of 180°(BDC) from Table 6-1; <u>a</u> is equal to <u>-1</u>, and <u>b</u> is equal to <u>0</u>.

$$PD = 1.74 \text{ in} \times \left(1 - (-1) + \frac{1.74 \text{ in}}{2 \times 5.7 \text{ in}} \times 0\right)$$

$$PD = 1.74 \text{ in} \times \left(1 + 1 + \frac{1.74 \text{ in}}{11.4 \text{ in}} \times 0\right)$$

PD = 1.74 in x (2 + 0.1526 x 0)

PD = 1.74 in x (2 + 0)

PD = 1.74 in x 2

PD = 3.48 in

And,

Cylinder Area = 12.56636 in²

Therefore,

Cylinder Volume = 12.56636 in² x 3.48 in

Cylinder Volume = 43.7309 in³ (cu in)

IF WE WERE TO MULTIPLY THE cylinder volume @ the **180°** crank angle times **eight**(*for an 8 cylinder engine*), the resulting or total cylinder volume of the engine will be **349.8472 cubic inches**. This is equal to the previously calculated engine displacement in Example(2b).

ALSO, NOTE THAT THE cylinder volume(cubic inch displacement) in **Examples(2a & 7g)** are equal.

FROM CLOSE OBSERVATION YOU CAN SEE the cylinder volume does not change by an equal amount for each **30°** **increment**(or any other increment) from TDC to BDC. This is because the cylinder volume like the piston displacement is affected by the crank throw and rod length.

YOU CAN ALSO SEE THAT AT **90°** of crankshaft rotation the cylinder volume(**25.202 cubic inches(in3)**) is not equal to **one-half(1/2)** of the cylinder's total displacement of **43.7309 in³** as one might think. The reason being is because the crank throw and rod length have an affect on the piston's displacement, and ultimately on the cylinder volume.

TABLE 7-1	
CRANK ANGLE(α) [in Degrees]	CYLINDER VOLUME (For a <u>5.7"</u> Rod Length & <u>1.74"</u> Crank Throw & <u>12.56636 in²</u> Cylinder Area)
0	0
1	0.0043
2	0.0174
3	0.0391
4	0.0695
5	0.1086
6	0.1562
7	0.2125
8	0.2774
9	0.3509
10	0.4328
11	0.5232
12	0.6221
13	0.7293
14	0.8448
15	0.9686
16	1.1006
17	1.2407
18	1.3889

TABLE 7-1	
CRANK ANGLE(α) [in Degrees]	CYLINDER VOLUME (For a 5.7" Rod Length & 1.74" Crank Throw & 12.56636 in^2 Cylinder Area)
19	1.545
20	1.709

TABLE 7-1	
CRANK ANGLE(α) [in Degrees]	CYLINDER VOLUME (For a 5.7" Rod Length & 1.74" Crank Throw & 12.56636 in^2 Cylinder Area)
21	1.8809
22	2.0605

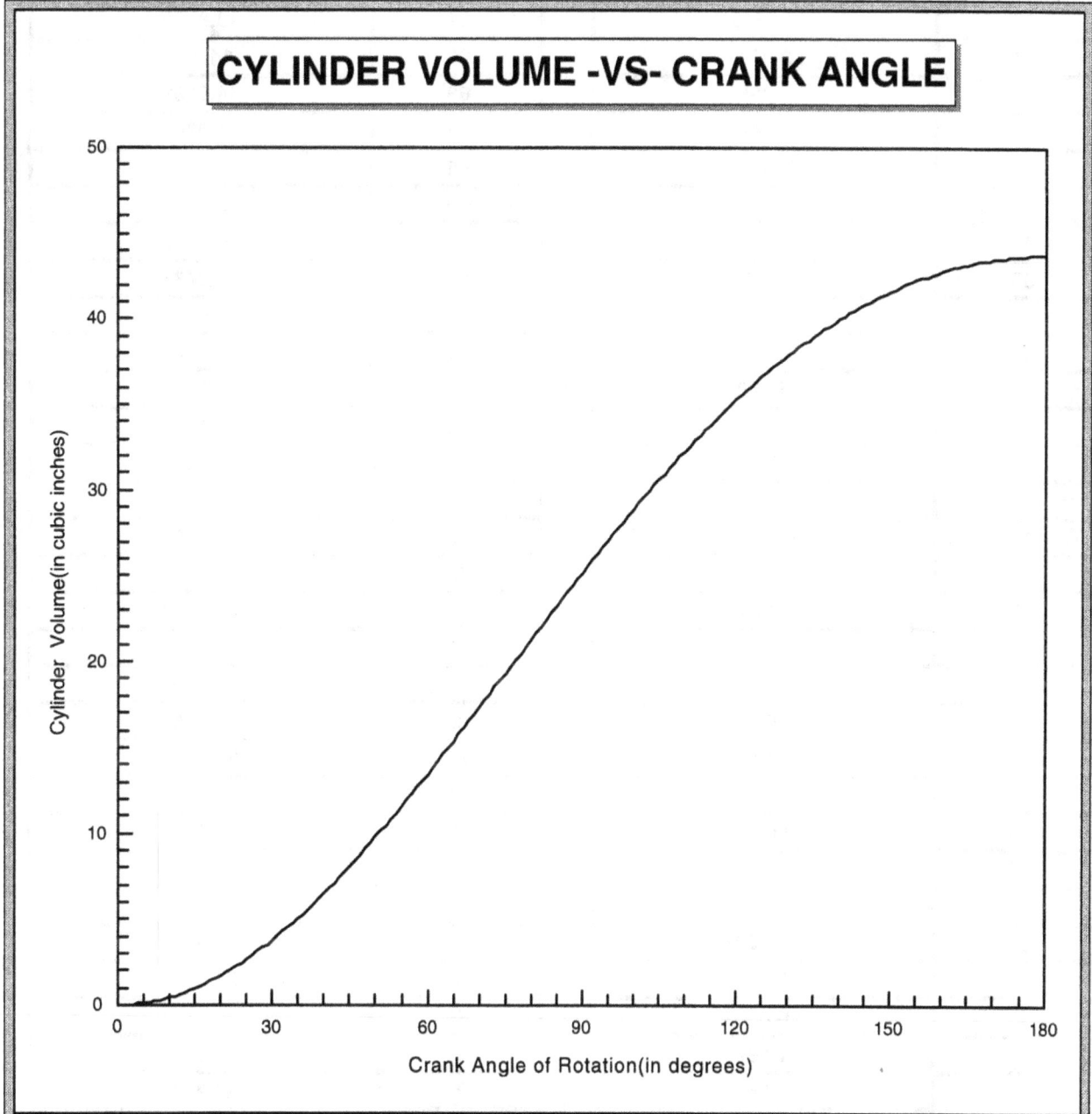

Figure 7-2: This graph of the data in Table 7-1 illustrates how cylinder volume above the piston increases from TDC(0° crank angle) to BDC(180° crank angle) for a 5.7" rod length, a 1.74" crank throw, and 12.56636 in^2 cylinder area.

CHAPTER SEVEN

TABLE 7-1	
CRANK ANGLE(α) [in Degrees]	CYLINDER VOLUME (For a 5.7" Rod Length & 1.74" Crank Throw & 12.56636 in² Cylinder Area)
23	2.2477
24	2.4425
25	2.6447
26	2.8543
27	3.071
28	3.295
29	3.5259
30	3.7638
31	4.0084
32	4.2597
33	4.5175
34	4.7818
35	5.0523
36	5.329
37	5.6117
38	5.9002
39	6.1945
40	6.4945
41	6.7998
42	7.1105
43	7.4264
44	7.7472
45	8.0729
46	8.4034
47	8.7383
48	9.0777
49	9.4213
50	9.7691
51	10.1207
52	10.4761
53	10.8351
54	11.1976
55	11.5634
56	11.9322
57	12.3041

TABLE 7-1	
CRANK ANGLE(α) [in Degrees]	CYLINDER VOLUME (For a 5.7" Rod Length & 1.74" Crank Throw & 12.56636 in² Cylinder Area)
58	12.6787
59	13.056
60	13.4358
61	13.8178
62	14.202
63	14.5883
64	14.9763
65	15.366
66	15.7572
67	16.1498
68	16.5435
69	16.9383
70	17.334
71	17.7304
72	18.1273
73	18.5247
74	18.9223
75	19.3201
76	19.7178
77	20.1153
78	20.5125
79	20.9092
80	21.3053
81	21.7006
82	22.0951
83	22.4885
84	22.8808
85	23.2718
86	23.6613
87	24.0493
88	24.4357
89	24.8202
90	25.2028
91	25.5834
92	25.9619

TABLE 7-1	
CRANK ANGLE(α) [in Degrees]	CYLINDER VOLUME (For a 5.7" Rod Length & 1.74" Crank Throw & 12.56636 in^2 Cylinder Area)
93	26.338
94	26.7118
95	27.0832
96	27.4519
97	27.818
98	28.1813
99	28.5417
100	28.8991
101	29.2534
102	29.6046
103	29.9526
104	30.2972
105	30.6385
106	30.9762
107	31.3104
108	31.6409
109	31.9678
110	32.2909
111	32.6101
112	32.9254
113	33.2368
114	33.5442
115	33.8475
116	34.1467
117	34.4417
118	34.7325
119	35.019
120	35.3012
121	35.5791
122	35.8526
123	36.1216
124	36.3863
125	36.6464
126	36.902
127	37.1531
128	37.3996
129	37.6415
130	37.8788
131	38.1114
132	38.3394
133	38.5628
134	38.7814
135	38.9954
136	39.2046
137	39.4091
138	39.6089
139	39.804
140	39.9943
141	40.1799
142	40.3607
143	40.5367
144	40.708
145	40.8746
146	41.0363
147	41.1934
148	41.3456
149	41.4931
150	41.6359
151	41.7738
152	41.9071
153	42.0356
154	42.1594
155	42.2784
156	42.3927
157	42.5023
158	42.6071
159	42.7072
160	42.8027
161	42.8934
162	42.9795

TABLE 7-1	
CRANK ANGLE(α) [in Degrees]	CYLINDER VOLUME (For a 5.7" Rod Length & 1.74" Crank Throw & 12.56636 in² Cylinder Area)
163	43.0608
164	43.1375
165	43.2094
166	43.2768
167	43.3394
168	43.3974
169	43.4507
170	43.4994
171	43.5434
172	43.5828
173	43.6175
174	43.6476
175	43.6731
176	43.6939
177	43.7101
178	43.7217
179	43.7286
180	43.7309

CHAPTER 8

AVERAGE PISTON *SPEED*

THIS ASPECT OF ENGINE OPERATION IS defined as the total displacement(distance traveled) by the piston during one complete revolution of the crankshaft times the engine speed.

THE HIGHER THE CRANKSHAFT rpm, the greater will be the piston speed. The varying directional speed of the piston and connecting rod assembly induces fatigue(repeated stress) within the rotating and reciprocating components. If the fatique stress limit is exceeded, parts failure could result, thus, possibly damaging the engine.

AS THE piston approaches top dead center(TDC) and/or bottom dead center(BDC), its velocity(speed) decreases. Therefore, the piston speed at TDC and BDC is zero. The piston then accelerates from both positions to its maximum speed at or near one-half (midway) the stroke.

A PISTON TRAVELS THROUGH a full or entire stroke after the completion of one-half(1/2) revolution of the crankshaft, and two times or twice the stroke at the completion of one(1) revolution of the crankshaft. Therefore, the average piston speed(in ft/min) for a specific or given RPM(engine speed) can be calculated from the following equation:

AVERAGE SPEED

$$\text{Avg Piston Speed} = \frac{2 \times \text{Stroke} \times \text{RPM} \times 1\text{ft}}{12 \text{ in}}$$

And,

Avg Piston Speed -- is the average piston speed calculated in feet per minute(ft/min)

RPM -- revolutions per minute(rev/min)

STROKE -- is measured in inches(in)

EXAMPLE(8):
Given: If an engine has a <u>3.48 in</u> stroke, and a crankshaft speed of 6000 RPM, the average piston speed will be...

$$\text{Avg Piston Speed} = \frac{2 \times \text{Stroke} \times \text{RPM} \times 1\text{ft}}{12\text{ in}}$$

$$\text{Avg Piston Speed} = \frac{2 \times 3.48\text{ in} \times 6000\text{ rpm} \times 1\text{ft}}{12\text{ in}}$$

$$\text{Avg Piston Speed} = \frac{6.96\text{ in} \times 6000\text{ rev/min} \times 1\text{ft}}{12\text{ in}}$$

$$\text{Avg Piston Speed} = \frac{41760\text{ ft/min}}{12}$$

$$\text{Avg Piston Speed} = 3480\text{ ft/min}$$

Note: The conversion factors of 1 ft & 12 in were included in order to convert the piston speed from in/min - to - ft/min.

To convert 3480 ft/min to ft/sec multiply by 1 min/60 sec, The result will be 58 ft/sec.

CLOSE EXAMINATION AND COMPARISON OF the graphs in Figures 8-1 & 8-2 reveals that as the crankshaft's stroke increases, the average piston speed will increase accordingly. This increase in the average piston speed is linear(increases the same amount) for each 100 rpm increment, and is represented hereafter -- in feet/minute -- by the data in Table 8-1.

THE AVERAGE PISTON SPEED IS VERY IMPORTANT IN THAT IT EXHIBITS whether the overall speed of an engine's pistons have increased or decreased as opposed to the speed of the pistons at any instant(instantaneous piston speed). The instantaneous piston speed is covered in chapter 9 of this volume.

TABLE 8-1

CRANKSHAFT SPEED [RPM]	STROKE	AVERAGE PISTON SPEED(1)	CRANKSHAFT SPEED [RPM]	STROKE	AVERAGE PISTON SPEED(2)
0	3.48	0	0	4	0
100	3.48	58	100	4	66.67
200	3.48	116	200	4	133.33
300	3.48	174	300	4	200
400	3.48	232	400	4	266.67
500	3.48	290	500	4	333.33
600	3.48	348	600	4	400
700	3.48	406	700	4	466.67
800	3.48	464	800	4	533.33
900	3.48	522	900	4	600
1000	3.48	580	1000	4	666.67
1100	3.48	638	1100	4	733.33
1200	3.48	696	1200	4	800
1300	3.48	754	1300	4	866.67
1400	3.48	812	1400	4	933.33
1500	3.48	870	1500	4	1000

TABLE 8-1						
CRANKSHAFT SPEED [RPM]	STROKE	AVERAGE PISTON SPEED(1)		CRANKSHAFT SPEED [RPM]	STROKE	AVERAGE PISTON SPEED(2)
1600	3.48	928		1600	4	1066.67
1700	3.48	986		1700	4	1133.33
1800	3.48	1044		1800	4	1200
1900	3.48	1102		1900	4	1266.67
2000	3.48	1160		2000	4	1333.33
2100	3.48	1218		2100	4	1400
2200	3.48	1276		2200	4	1466.67
2300	3.48	1334		2300	4	1533.33
2400	3.48	1392		2400	4	1600
2500	3.48	1450		2500	4	1666.67
2600	3.48	1508		2600	4	1733.33
2700	3.48	1566		2700	4	1800
2800	3.48	1624		2800	4	1866.67
2900	3.48	1682		2900	4	1933.33
3000	3.48	1740		3000	4	2000
3100	3.48	1798		3100	4	2066.67
3200	3.48	1856		3200	4	2133.33
3300	3.48	1914		3300	4	2200
3400	3.48	1972		3400	4	2266.67
3500	3.48	2030		3500	4	2333.33
3600	3.48	2088		3600	4	2400
3700	3.48	2146		3700	4	2466.67
3800	3.48	2204		3800	4	2533.33
3900	3.48	2262		3900	4	2600
4000	3.48	2320		4000	4	2666.67
4100	3.48	2378		4100	4	2733.33
4200	3.48	2436		4200	4	2800
4300	3.48	2494		4300	4	2866.67
4400	3.48	2552		4400	4	2933.33
4500	3.48	2610		4500	4	3000
4600	3.48	2668		4600	4	3066.67
4700	3.48	2726		4700	4	3133.33
4800	3.48	2784		4800	4	3200
4900	3.48	2842		4900	4	3266.67

TABLE 8-1						
CRANKSHAFT SPEED [RPM]	STROKE	AVERAGE PISTON SPEED(1)		CRANKSHAFT SPEED [RPM]	STROKE	AVERAGE PISTON SPEED(2)
5000	3.48	2900		5000	4	3333.33
5100	3.48	2958		5100	4	3400
5200	3.48	3016		5200	4	3466.67
5300	3.48	3074		5300	4	3533.33
5400	3.48	3132		5400	4	3600
5500	3.48	3190		5500	4	3666.67
5600	3.48	3248		5600	4	3733.33
5700	3.48	3306		5700	4	3800
5800	3.48	3364		5800	4	3866.67
5900	3.48	3422		5900	4	3933.33
6000	3.48	3480		6000	4	4000

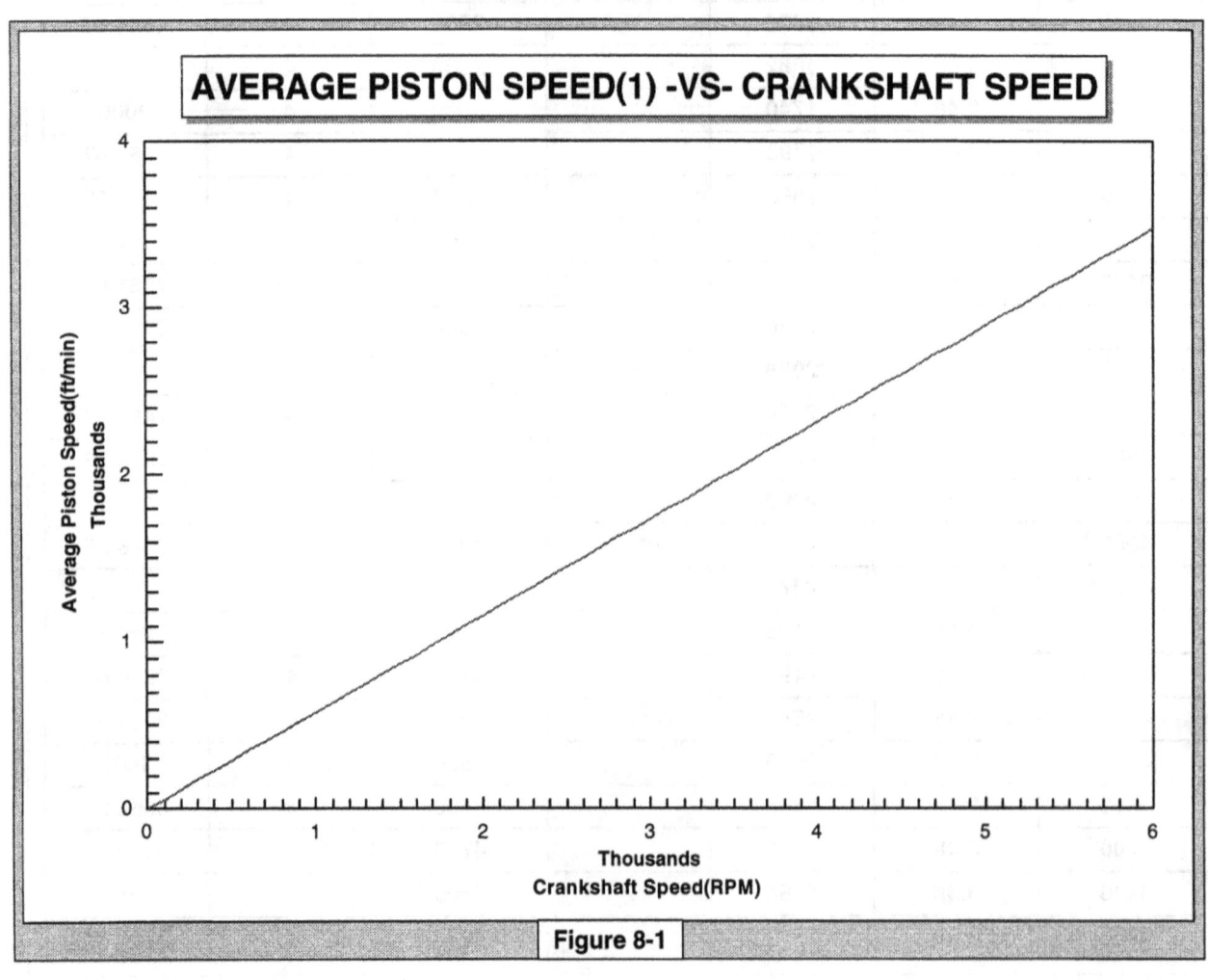

Figure 8-1

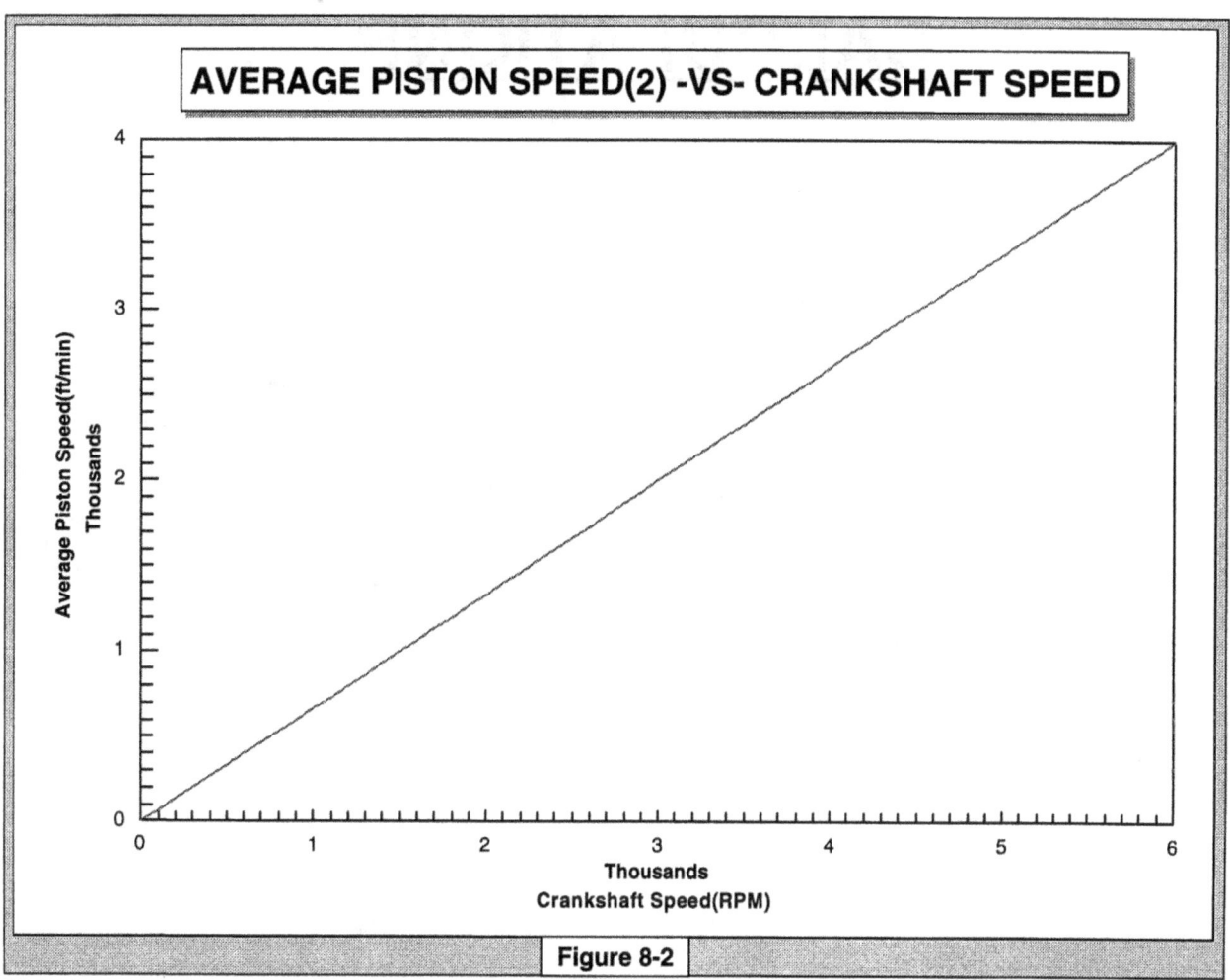

Figure 8-2

CHAPTER EIGHT

CALCULATIONS

CHAPTER 9

INSTANTANEOUS PISTON SPEED

UNLIKE THE AVERAGE PISTON SPEED -- which is determined by the crankshaft's stroke and the engine speed -- the *instantaneous piston speed or velocity* can be calculated at any crank angle or any instant(infinitesimal change in time). This is provided that the engine speed is known during this angle of displacement or instant(see Illustration 9-1).

A THOROUGH EXPLORATION OF THIS variable will denote its relationship to valve timing and the rate of valve movement that affects the incoming air-fuel mixture and valve-to-piston clearances.

AT TIMES IT MAY BE HARD TO PHANTOM THE velocity or motion of the piston in such brevity of time(as related to the engine's crankshaft speed). Yet, this is of extreme importance when anyone is in search of, or seeking to achieve the optimum engine performance

THE EQUATION FOR THE instantaneous piston speed is ...

$$\text{IPS} = \text{Crankpin Veloc} \times \left[c + \frac{\text{Crank Throw}}{2 \times \text{Rod length}} \times d \right]$$

> **Unlike The Average Piston Speed...The Instantaneous Piston Speed Or Velocity Can Be Calculated At Any Crank Angle Or Any Instant...**

Where,

IPS -- Instantaneous Piston Speed

Crankpin Veloc -- the crankpin velocity calculated in feet per second (ft/sec)

- **c** -- is the sin(pronounced -- sine) of the crank angle(α) and is given in Table 9-1

- **d** -- is the sin(pronounced -- sine) of two times the crank angle(α) [i.e. - $\sin(2\alpha)$] and is given in Table 9-1

Crank Throw -- given in inches(in)

Rod Length -- given in inches(in)

rad -- radians

> Crankpin Angular Veloc = 6.283 rad x Crankshaft rpm(radians/min)

> Crankpin Velocity = Crank Throw x Crankpin Angular Velocity(ft/min)

EXAMPLE(9a):
Using the previous data from EXAMPLE(8a) where the chosen peak engine speed is 6000 rpm. The instantaneous piston speed for a crank angle of (a) 106° ATDC when the intake valve has reached its maximum lift, (b) 76° ABDC when the intake valve is fully closed, and (c) 44° BTDC when the intake valve just begins to open.

> Crankpin Angular Veloc = 6.283 rad x Crankshaft rpm(radians/min)

> Crankpin Angular Veloc = 6.283 rad x 6000 rev/min

> Crankpin Angular Veloc = 37698 rad/min

Crank Throw = 1.74 in
Crank Throw = 1.74 in /(12 in/ft) = .145 ft

Rod Length = 5.7 in

Therefore,

> Crankpin Velocity = Crank Throw x Crankpin Angular Velocity(ft/min)

> Crankpin Velocity = .145 ft x 37698 rad/min

> Crankpin Velocity = 5466.21 ft/min

-Also-

> Crankpin Velocity = 5466.21 ft/min x (1 min/60)

> Crankpin Velocity = 91.104 ft/sec

Now,

For a crank angle(α) of 106° ATDC from Table 9-2 starting on page; c is equal to -0.6947, and d is equal to -0.9994.

> IPS = Crankpin Veloc x [c + $\frac{\text{Crank Throw}}{2 \times \text{Rod length}}$ x d]

IPS = 91.104 ft/sec x [.9613 + $\frac{1.74 \text{ in}}{2 \times 5.7 \text{ in}}$ x (-.5299)]

IPS = 91.104 ft/sec x [.9613 + $\frac{1.74 \text{ in}}{11.4 \text{ in}}$ x (-.5299)]

IPS = 91.104 ft/sec x [.9613 + .1526 x (-.5299)]

IPS = 91.104 ft/sec x [.9613 + (-.0809)]

IPS = 91.104 ft/sec x [.8804]

IPS = 80.208 ft/sec

EXAMPLE(9b):
For α = 76° ABDC, this signifies that the piston has traveled from top dead center (TDC) to bottom dead center (BDC) and is now ascending from BDC back toward TDC. In other words, the crankshaft has rotated 180° (one-half revolution) from TDC to BDC, and 76° from BDC toward TDC.

Therefore,

α = 180° + 76° = 256°

For a crank angle(α) of 76° ABDC or 256° from Table 9-2; c is equal to -0.9703, and d is equal to 0.4695.

IPS = 91.104 ft/sec x [-.9703 + $\frac{1.74 \text{ in}}{11.4 \text{ in}}$ x (.4695)]

IPS = 91.104 ft/sec x [-.9703 + .1526 x (.4695)]

IPS = 91.104 ft/sec x [-.9703 + (.0716)]

IPS = 91.104 ft/sec x [-.8986]

IPS = -81.866 ft/sec

EXAMPLE(9c):

For α = 44° **BTDC**, this means the crankshaft has rotated 180° from TDC-to-BDC, and has rotated from BDC to the point where it is 44° from completing one full revolution of operation or from TDC.

Since one full revolution is equivalent to 360°, the crank angle can be expressed as...

α = 360° - 44°   - or -
α = 1/2 revolution + (1/2 revolution - 44°)
α = 180° + (180° - 44°) = 180° + 136° = 316°

For a crank angle(α) of 44° **BTDC** or 316° from Table 9-2; **c** is equal to **-0.6947**, and **d** is equal to **-0.9994**.

So,

IPS = 91.104 ft/sec x [-.6947 + $\frac{1.74 \text{ in}}{11.4 \text{ in}}$ x (-.9994)]

IPS = 91.104 ft/sec x [-.6947 + .1526 x (-.9994)]

IPS = 91.104 ft/sec x [-.6947 + (-.1525)]

IPS = 91.104 ft/sec x [-.8472]

IPS = -77.183 ft/sec

IN COMPARISON TO THE AVERAGE PISTON speed, it is evident from Table 9-1 for a given engine speed(rpm), the piston's velocity changes with respect to the crank angle and does not remain constant as it is set in motion from TDC to BDC.

IN THE FIRST PART(EXAMPLE 9a), NOTICE THAT the piston speed is increasing and is positive(+) because the piston is moving in a positive direction away from TDC toward BDC(see Table 9-1).

IN THE SECOND PART(EXAMPLE 9b) the piston speed is increasing and is negative(-) because the piston is moving in a negative direction away from BDC(see Table 9-1).

IN THE LAST PART(C), the piston speed is decreasing and is negative(-) because the piston is moving in the opposite or negative direction away from BDC toward TDC(see Table 9-1).

*ALSO, note that the piston's velocity is and will be zero at **TDC(0° or 360°)** & **BDC(180°)** for any engine speed, stroke, and rod length because the piston has to stop and change directions(see Figure 9-1). At **90°** and **270°** of crankshaft rotation the piston speed is equal to the crank throw speed or velocity for this and any engine combination.*

EVEN THOUGH THE maximum valve lift occurs at **106° ATDC** in **EXAMPLE(9a)**, the maximum piston speed occurs at **75° ATDC** and at **285°** which is equal to **75° BTDC(see Table 9-1)**. This is because the point where the maximum piston speed occurs depends on the engine's crank throw and rod length and not on valve timing.

KEEP IN MIND THAT the longer a connecting rod is, the slower the piston will move away from top dead center; and the faster it will move away from bottom dead center. This is true at any engine speed, when compared to an engine with a shorter connecting rod utilizing the same stroke.

OTHER VALUES FOR **c** and **d** at any crank angle can be found in **Table 9-2**.

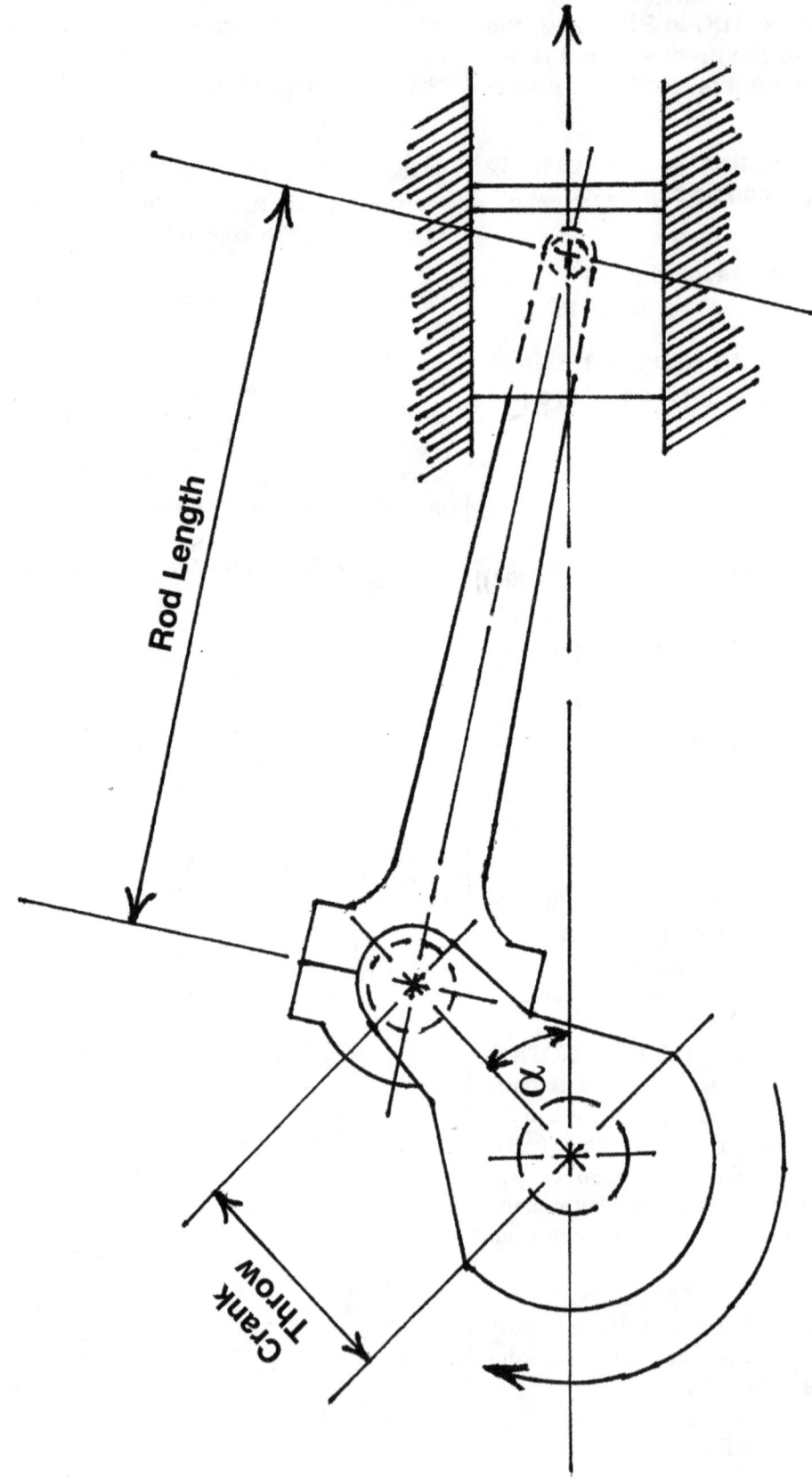

Illustration 9-1

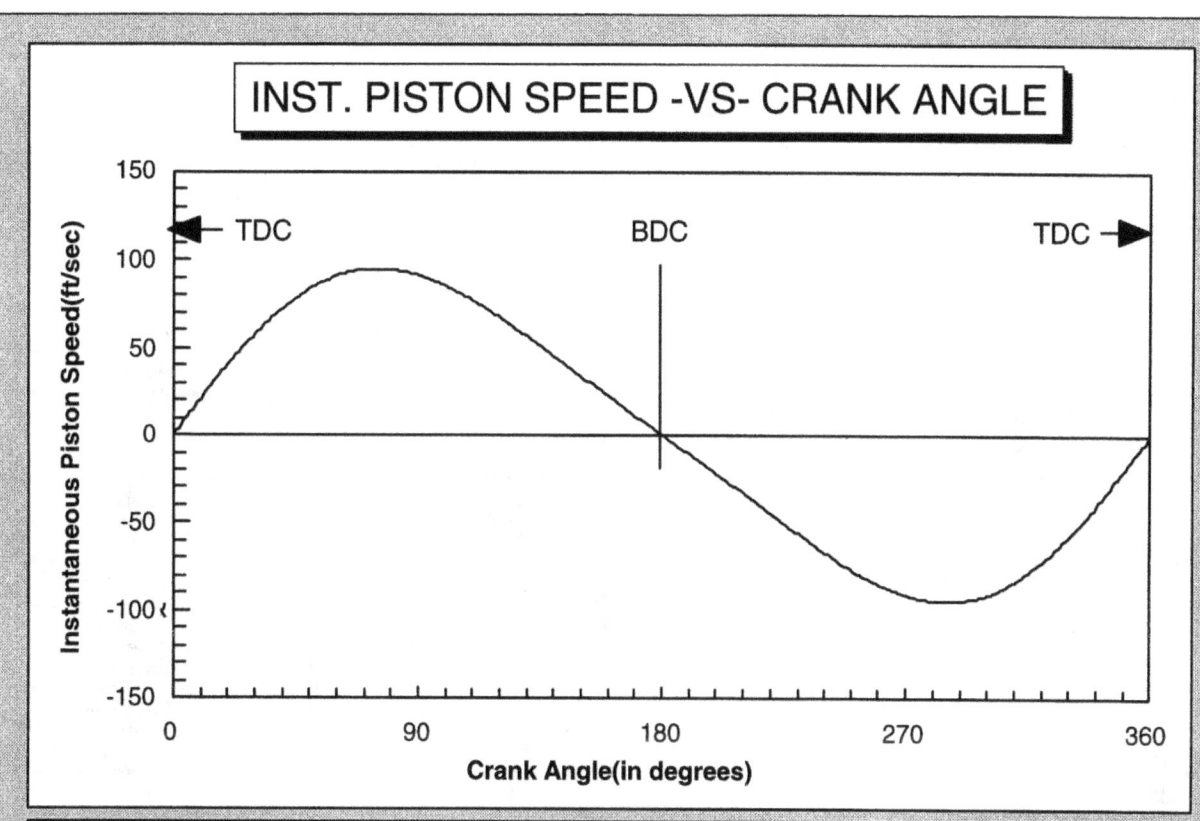

Figure 9-1: The piston speed at TDC(0° & 360°) and BDC(180°) will always be zero, and the maximum piston speed does not always occur at 90°(1/4 of a revolution) and 270°(3/4 of a revolution) as shown above. At 90° and 270° the piston speed is also equal to the crank throw speed or velocity.

TABLE 9-1			TABLE 9-1		
CRANK ANGLE(α) [in Degrees]	STROKE / ROD LENGTH	INSTANTANEOUS PISTON SPEED	CRANK ANGLE(α) [in Degrees]	STROKE / ROD LENGTH	INSTANTANEOUS PISTON SPEED
0	3.48 / 5.7	0	11	3.48 / 5.7	22.5925
1	3.48 / 5.7	2.0753	12	3.48 / 5.7	24.5974
2	3.48 / 5.7	4.1495	13	3.48 / 5.7	26.5896
3	3.48 / 5.7	6.2215	14	3.48 / 5.7	28.5682
4	3.48 / 5.7	8.2903	15	3.48 / 5.7	30.5321
5	3.48 / 5.7	10.3549	16	3.48 / 5.7	32.4804
6	3.48 / 5.7	12.414	17	3.48 / 5.7	34.412
7	3.48 / 5.7	14.4668	18	3.48 / 5.7	36.326
8	3.48 / 5.7	16.5121	19	3.48 / 5.7	38.2215
9	3.48 / 5.7	18.5488	20	3.48 / 5.7	40.0976
10	3.48 / 5.7	20.576	21	3.48 / 5.7	41.9532

TABLE 9-1		
CRANK ANGLE(α) [in Degrees]	STROKE / ROD LENGTH	INSTANTANEOUS PISTON SPEED
22	3.48 / 5.7	43.7876
23	3.48 / 5.7	45.5998
24	3.48 / 5.7	47.389
25	3.48 / 5.7	49.1543
26	3.48 / 5.7	50.8949
27	3.48 / 5.7	52.61
28	3.48 / 5.7	54.2988
29	3.48 / 5.7	55.9605
30	3.48 / 5.7	57.5944
31	3.48 / 5.7	59.1997
32	3.48 / 5.7	60.7758
33	3.48 / 5.7	62.322
34	3.48 / 5.7	63.8375
35	3.48 / 5.7	65.3219
36	3.48 / 5.7	66.7744
37	3.48 / 5.7	68.1944
38	3.48 / 5.7	69.5815
39	3.48 / 5.7	70.9351
40	3.48 / 5.7	72.2546
41	3.48 / 5.7	73.5396
42	3.48 / 5.7	74.7896
43	3.48 / 5.7	76.0043
44	3.48 / 5.7	77.183
45	3.48 / 5.7	78.3256
46	3.48 / 5.7	79.4316
47	3.48 / 5.7	80.5007
48	3.48 / 5.7	81.5326
49	3.48 / 5.7	82.5271
50	3.48 / 5.7	83.4838
51	3.48 / 5.7	84.4026
52	3.48 / 5.7	85.2832
53	3.48 / 5.7	86.1256
54	3.48 / 5.7	86.9295
55	3.48 / 5.7	87.6948
56	3.48 / 5.7	88.4215
57	3.48 / 5.7	89.1094
58	3.48 / 5.7	89.7586
59	3.48 / 5.7	90.3691
60	3.48 / 5.7	90.9408
61	3.48 / 5.7	91.4738
62	3.48 / 5.7	91.9681
63	3.48 / 5.7	92.4239
64	3.48 / 5.7	92.8413
65	3.48 / 5.7	93.2204
66	3.48 / 5.7	93.5613
67	3.48 / 5.7	93.8643
68	3.48 / 5.7	94.1296
69	3.48 / 5.7	94.3574
70	3.48 / 5.7	94.5479
71	3.48 / 5.7	94.7015
72	3.48 / 5.7	94.8184
73	3.48 / 5.7	94.899
74	3.48 / 5.7	94.9435
75	3.48 / 5.7	94.9524
76	3.48 / 5.7	94.926
77	3.48 / 5.7	94.8647
78	3.48 / 5.7	94.769
79	3.48 / 5.7	94.6392
80	3.48 / 5.7	94.4758
81	3.48 / 5.7	94.2793
82	3.48 / 5.7	94.0502
83	3.48 / 5.7	93.7889
84	3.48 / 5.7	93.496
85	3.48 / 5.7	93.172
86	3.48 / 5.7	92.8173
87	3.48 / 5.7	92.4326
88	3.48 / 5.7	92.0185
89	3.48 / 5.7	91.5754
90	3.48 / 5.7	91.104
91	3.48 / 5.7	90.6048

TABLE 9-1		
CRANK ANGLE(α) [in Degrees]	STROKE / ROD LENGTH	INSTANTANEOUS PISTON SPEED
92	3.48 / 5.7	90.0785
93	3.48 / 5.7	89.5256
94	3.48 / 5.7	88.9468
95	3.48 / 5.7	88.3427
96	3.48 / 5.7	87.7138
97	3.48 / 5.7	87.0609
98	3.48 / 5.7	86.3845
99	3.48 / 5.7	85.6854
100	3.48 / 5.7	84.964
101	3.48 / 5.7	84.2211
102	3.48 / 5.7	83.4573
103	3.48 / 5.7	82.6733
104	3.48 / 5.7	81.8697
105	3.48 / 5.7	81.047
106	3.48 / 5.7	80.2061
107	3.48 / 5.7	79.3474
108	3.48 / 5.7	78.4717
109	3.48 / 5.7	77.5795
110	3.48 / 5.7	76.6716
111	3.48 / 5.7	75.7484
112	3.48 / 5.7	74.8107
113	3.48 / 5.7	73.859
114	3.48 / 5.7	72.894
115	3.48 / 5.7	71.9162
116	3.48 / 5.7	70.9262
117	3.48 / 5.7	69.9246
118	3.48 / 5.7	68.912
119	3.48 / 5.7	67.889
120	3.48 / 5.7	66.856
121	3.48 / 5.7	65.8137
122	3.48 / 5.7	64.7625
123	3.48 / 5.7	63.7031
124	3.48 / 5.7	62.6358
125	3.48 / 5.7	61.5613
126	3.48 / 5.7	60.4799
127	3.48 / 5.7	59.3922
128	3.48 / 5.7	58.2986
129	3.48 / 5.7	57.1996
130	3.48 / 5.7	56.0956
131	3.48 / 5.7	54.987
132	3.48 / 5.7	53.8743
133	3.48 / 5.7	52.7578
134	3.48 / 5.7	51.6379
135	3.48 / 5.7	50.5149
136	3.48 / 5.7	49.3893
137	3.48 / 5.7	48.2613
138	3.48 / 5.7	47.1313
139	3.48 / 5.7	45.9996
140	3.48 / 5.7	44.8664
141	3.48 / 5.7	43.7321
142	3.48 / 5.7	42.5969
143	3.48 / 5.7	41.4611
144	3.48 / 5.7	40.3248
145	3.48 / 5.7	39.1884
146	3.48 / 5.7	38.0519
147	3.48 / 5.7	36.9156
148	3.48 / 5.7	35.7797
149	3.48 / 5.7	34.6443
150	3.48 / 5.7	33.5096
151	3.48 / 5.7	32.3757
152	3.48 / 5.7	31.2427
153	3.48 / 5.7	30.1107
154	3.48 / 5.7	28.9798
155	3.48 / 5.7	27.8501
156	3.48 / 5.7	26.7216
157	3.48 / 5.7	25.5945
158	3.48 / 5.7	24.4687
159	3.48 / 5.7	23.3443
160	3.48 / 5.7	22.2212
161	3.48 / 5.7	21.0996

TABLE 9-1		
CRANK ANGLE(α) [in Degrees]	STROKE / ROD LENGTH	INSTANTANEOUS PISTON SPEED
162	3.48 / 5.7	19.9793
163	3.48 / 5.7	18.8605
164	3.48 / 5.7	17.743
165	3.48 / 5.7	16.6268
166	3.48 / 5.7	15.5119
167	3.48 / 5.7	14.3982
168	3.48 / 5.7	13.2858
169	3.48 / 5.7	12.1744
170	3.48 / 5.7	11.0641
171	3.48 / 5.7	9.9548
172	3.48 / 5.7	8.8464
173	3.48 / 5.7	7.7388
174	3.48 / 5.7	6.6319
175	3.48 / 5.7	5.5256
176	3.48 / 5.7	4.4198
177	3.48 / 5.7	3.3145
178	3.48 / 5.7	2.2095
179	3.48 / 5.7	1.1047
180	3.48 / 5.7	0
181	3.48 / 5.7	-1.1047
182	3.48 / 5.7	-2.2095
183	3.48 / 5.7	-3.3145
184	3.48 / 5.7	-4.4198
185	3.48 / 5.7	-5.5256
186	3.48 / 5.7	-6.6319
187	3.48 / 5.7	-7.7388
188	3.48 / 5.7	-8.8464
189	3.48 / 5.7	-9.9548
190	3.48 / 5.7	-11.0641
191	3.48 / 5.7	-12.1744
192	3.48 / 5.7	-13.2858
193	3.48 / 5.7	-14.3982
194	3.48 / 5.7	-15.5119
195	3.48 / 5.7	-16.6268
196	3.48 / 5.7	-17.743
197	3.48 / 5.7	-18.8605
198	3.48 / 5.7	-19.9793
199	3.48 / 5.7	-21.0996
200	3.48 / 5.7	-22.2212
201	3.48 / 5.7	-23.3443
202	3.48 / 5.7	-24.4687
203	3.48 / 5.7	-25.5945
204	3.48 / 5.7	-26.7216
205	3.48 / 5.7	-27.8501
206	3.48 / 5.7	-28.9798
207	3.48 / 5.7	-30.1107
208	3.48 / 5.7	-31.2427
209	3.48 / 5.7	-32.3757
210	3.48 / 5.7	-33.5096
211	3.48 / 5.7	-34.6443
212	3.48 / 5.7	-35.7797
213	3.48 / 5.7	-36.9156
214	3.48 / 5.7	-38.0519
215	3.48 / 5.7	-39.1884
216	3.48 / 5.7	-40.3248
217	3.48 / 5.7	-41.4611
218	3.48 / 5.7	-42.5969
219	3.48 / 5.7	-43.7321
220	3.48 / 5.7	-44.8664
221	3.48 / 5.7	-45.9996
222	3.48 / 5.7	-47.1313
223	3.48 / 5.7	-48.2613
224	3.48 / 5.7	-49.3893
225	3.48 / 5.7	-50.5149
226	3.48 / 5.7	-51.6379
227	3.48 / 5.7	-52.7578
228	3.48 / 5.7	-53.8743
229	3.48 / 5.7	-54.987
230	3.48 / 5.7	-56.0956
231	3.48 / 5.7	-57.1996

TABLE 9-1		
CRANK ANGLE(α) [in Degrees]	STROKE / ROD LENGTH	INSTANTANEOUS PISTON SPEED
232	3.48 / 5.7	-58.2986
233	3.48 / 5.7	-59.3922
234	3.48 / 5.7	-60.4799
235	3.48 / 5.7	-61.5613
236	3.48 / 5.7	-62.6358
237	3.48 / 5.7	-63.7031
238	3.48 / 5.7	-64.7625
239	3.48 / 5.7	-65.8137
240	3.48 / 5.7	-66.856
241	3.48 / 5.7	-67.889
242	3.48 / 5.7	-68.912
243	3.48 / 5.7	-69.9246
244	3.48 / 5.7	-70.9262
245	3.48 / 5.7	-71.9162
246	3.48 / 5.7	-72.894
247	3.48 / 5.7	-73.859
248	3.48 / 5.7	-74.8107
249	3.48 / 5.7	-75.7484
250	3.48 / 5.7	-76.6716
251	3.48 / 5.7	-77.5795
252	3.48 / 5.7	-78.4717
253	3.48 / 5.7	-79.3474
254	3.48 / 5.7	-80.2061
255	3.48 / 5.7	-81.047
256	3.48 / 5.7	-81.8697
257	3.48 / 5.7	-82.6733
258	3.48 / 5.7	-83.4573
259	3.48 / 5.7	-84.2211
260	3.48 / 5.7	-84.964
261	3.48 / 5.7	-85.6854
262	3.48 / 5.7	-86.3845
263	3.48 / 5.7	-87.0609
264	3.48 / 5.7	-87.7138
265	3.48 / 5.7	-88.3427
266	3.48 / 5.7	-88.9468
267	3.48 / 5.7	-89.5256
268	3.48 / 5.7	-90.0785
269	3.48 / 5.7	-90.6048
270	3.48 / 5.7	-91.104
271	3.48 / 5.7	-91.5754
272	3.48 / 5.7	-92.0185
273	3.48 / 5.7	-92.4326
274	3.48 / 5.7	-92.8173
275	3.48 / 5.7	-93.172
276	3.48 / 5.7	-93.496
277	3.48 / 5.7	-93.7889
278	3.48 / 5.7	-94.0502
279	3.48 / 5.7	-94.2793
280	3.48 / 5.7	-94.4758
281	3.48 / 5.7	-94.6392
282	3.48 / 5.7	-94.769
283	3.48 / 5.7	-94.8647
284	3.48 / 5.7	-94.926
285	3.48 / 5.7	-94.9524
286	3.48 / 5.7	-94.9435
287	3.48 / 5.7	-94.899
288	3.48 / 5.7	-94.8184
289	3.48 / 5.7	-94.7015
290	3.48 / 5.7	-94.5479
291	3.48 / 5.7	-94.3574
292	3.48 / 5.7	-94.1296
293	3.48 / 5.7	-93.8643
294	3.48 / 5.7	-93.5613
295	3.48 / 5.7	-93.2204
296	3.48 / 5.7	-92.8413
297	3.48 / 5.7	-92.4239
298	3.48 / 5.7	-91.9681
299	3.48 / 5.7	-91.4738
300	3.48 / 5.7	-90.9408
301	3.48 / 5.7	-90.3691

TABLE 9-1		
CRANK ANGLE(α) [in Degrees]	STROKE / ROD LENGTH	INSTANTANEOUS PISTON SPEED
302	3.48 / 5.7	-89.7586
303	3.48 / 5.7	-89.1094
304	3.48 / 5.7	-88.4215
305	3.48 / 5.7	-87.6948
306	3.48 / 5.7	-86.9295
307	3.48 / 5.7	-86.1256
308	3.48 / 5.7	-85.2832
309	3.48 / 5.7	-84.4026
310	3.48 / 5.7	-83.4838
311	3.48 / 5.7	-82.5271
312	3.48 / 5.7	-81.5326
313	3.48 / 5.7	-80.5007
314	3.48 / 5.7	-79.4316
315	3.48 / 5.7	-78.3256
316	3.48 / 5.7	-77.183
317	3.48 / 5.7	-76.0043
318	3.48 / 5.7	-74.7896
319	3.48 / 5.7	-73.5396
320	3.48 / 5.7	-72.2546
321	3.48 / 5.7	-70.9351
322	3.48 / 5.7	-69.5815
323	3.48 / 5.7	-68.1944
324	3.48 / 5.7	-66.7744
325	3.48 / 5.7	-65.3219
326	3.48 / 5.7	-63.8375
327	3.48 / 5.7	-62.322
328	3.48 / 5.7	-60.7758
329	3.48 / 5.7	-59.1997
330	3.48 / 5.7	-57.5944
331	3.48 / 5.7	-55.9605
332	3.48 / 5.7	-54.2988
333	3.48 / 5.7	-52.61
334	3.48 / 5.7	-50.8949
335	3.48 / 5.7	-49.1543
336	3.48 / 5.7	-47.389

TABLE 9-1		
CRANK ANGLE(α) [in Degrees]	STROKE / ROD LENGTH	INSTANTANEOUS PISTON SPEED
337	3.48 / 5.7	-45.5998
338	3.48 / 5.7	-43.7876
339	3.48 / 5.7	-41.9532
340	3.48 / 5.7	-40.0976
341	3.48 / 5.7	-38.2215
342	3.48 / 5.7	-36.326
343	3.48 / 5.7	-34.412
344	3.48 / 5.7	-32.4804
345	3.48 / 5.7	-30.5321
346	3.48 / 5.7	-28.5682
347	3.48 / 5.7	-26.5896
348	3.48 / 5.7	-24.5974
349	3.48 / 5.7	-22.5925
350	3.48 / 5.7	-20.576
351	3.48 / 5.7	-18.5488
352	3.48 / 5.7	-16.5121
353	3.48 / 5.7	-14.4668
354	3.48 / 5.7	-12.414
355	3.48 / 5.7	-10.3549
356	3.48 / 5.7	-8.2903
357	3.48 / 5.7	-6.2215
358	3.48 / 5.7	-4.1495
359	3.48 / 5.7	-2.0753
360	3.48 / 5.7	0

TABLE 9-2		
CRANK ANGLE(α) [in Degrees]	c	d
0	0	0
1	0.0175	0.0349
2	0.0349	0.0698
3	0.0523	0.1045
4	0.0698	0.1392
5	0.0872	0.1736
6	0.1045	0.2079
7	0.1219	0.2419
8	0.1392	0.2756
9	0.1564	0.309
10	0.1736	0.342
11	0.1908	0.3746
12	0.2079	0.4067
13	0.225	0.4384
14	0.2419	0.4695
15	0.2588	0.5
16	0.2756	0.5299
17	0.2924	0.5592
18	0.309	0.5878
19	0.3256	0.6157
20	0.342	0.6428
21	0.3584	0.6691
22	0.3746	0.6947
23	0.3907	0.7193
24	0.4067	0.7431
25	0.4226	0.766
26	0.4384	0.788
27	0.454	0.809
28	0.4695	0.829
29	0.4848	0.848
30	0.5	0.866
31	0.515	0.8829
32	0.5299	0.8988
33	0.5446	0.9135
34	0.5592	0.9272
35	0.5736	0.9397
36	0.5878	0.9511
37	0.6018	0.9613
38	0.6157	0.9703
39	0.6293	0.9781
40	0.6428	0.9848
41	0.6561	0.9903
42	0.6691	0.9945
43	0.682	0.9976
44	0.6947	0.9994
45	0.7071	1
46	0.7193	0.9994
47	0.7314	0.9976
48	0.7431	0.9945
49	0.7547	0.9903
50	0.766	0.9848
51	0.7771	0.9781
52	0.788	0.9703
53	0.7986	0.9613
54	0.809	0.9511
55	0.8192	0.9397
56	0.829	0.9272
57	0.8387	0.9135
58	0.848	0.8988
59	0.8572	0.8829
60	0.866	0.866
61	0.8746	0.848
62	0.8829	0.829
63	0.891	0.809
64	0.8988	0.788
65	0.9063	0.766
66	0.9135	0.7431
67	0.9205	0.7193
68	0.9272	0.6947
69	0.9336	0.6691
70	0.9397	0.6428
71	0.9455	0.6157

TABLE 9-2

CRANK ANGLE(α) [in Degrees]	c	d
72	0.9511	0.5878
73	0.9563	0.5592
74	0.9613	0.5299
75	0.9659	0.5
76	0.9703	0.4695
77	0.9744	0.4384
78	0.9781	0.4067
79	0.9816	0.3746
80	0.9848	0.342
81	0.9877	0.309
82	0.9903	0.2756
83	0.9925	0.2419
84	0.9945	0.2079
85	0.9962	0.1736
86	0.9976	0.1392
87	0.9986	0.1045
88	0.9994	0.0698
89	0.9998	0.0349
90	1	0
91	0.9998	-0.0349
92	0.9994	-0.0698
93	0.9986	-0.1045
94	0.9976	-0.1392
95	0.9962	-0.1736
96	0.9945	-0.2079
97	0.9925	-0.2419
98	0.9903	-0.2756
99	0.9877	-0.309
100	0.9848	-0.342
101	0.9816	-0.3746
102	0.9781	-0.4067
103	0.9744	-0.4384
104	0.9703	-0.4695
105	0.9659	-0.5
106	0.9613	-0.5299
107	0.9563	-0.5592
108	0.9511	-0.5878
109	0.9455	-0.6157
110	0.9397	-0.6428
111	0.9336	-0.6691
112	0.9272	-0.6947
113	0.9205	-0.7193
114	0.9135	-0.7431
115	0.9063	-0.766
116	0.8988	-0.788
117	0.891	-0.809
118	0.8829	-0.829
119	0.8746	-0.848
120	0.866	-0.866
121	0.8572	-0.8829
122	0.848	-0.8988
123	0.8387	-0.9135
124	0.829	-0.9272
125	0.8192	-0.9397
126	0.809	-0.9511
127	0.7986	-0.9613
128	0.788	-0.9703
129	0.7771	-0.9781
130	0.766	-0.9848
131	0.7547	-0.9903
132	0.7431	-0.9945
133	0.7314	-0.9976
134	0.7193	-0.9994
135	0.7071	-1
136	0.6947	-0.9994
137	0.682	-0.9976
138	0.6691	-0.9945
139	0.6561	-0.9903
140	0.6428	-0.9848
141	0.6293	-0.9781
142	0.6157	-0.9703
143	0.6018	-0.9613

TABLE 9-2		
CRANK ANGLE(α) [in Degrees]	c	d
144	0.5878	-0.9511
145	0.5736	-0.9397
146	0.5592	-0.9272
147	0.5446	-0.9135
148	0.5299	-0.8988
149	0.515	-0.8829
150	0.5	-0.866
151	0.4848	-0.848
152	0.4695	-0.829
153	0.454	-0.809
154	0.4384	-0.788
155	0.4226	-0.766
156	0.4067	-0.7431
157	0.3907	-0.7193
158	0.3746	-0.6947
159	0.3584	-0.6691
160	0.342	-0.6428
161	0.3256	-0.6157
162	0.309	-0.5878
163	0.2924	-0.5592
164	0.2756	-0.5299
165	0.2588	-0.5
166	0.2419	-0.4695
167	0.225	-0.4384
168	0.2079	-0.4067
169	0.1908	-0.3746
170	0.1736	-0.342
171	0.1564	-0.309
172	0.1392	-0.2756
173	0.1219	-0.2419
174	0.1045	-0.2079
175	0.0872	-0.1736
176	0.0698	-0.1392
177	0.0523	-0.1045
178	0.0349	-0.0698
179	0.0175	-0.0349

TABLE 9-2		
CRANK ANGLE(α) [in Degrees]	c	d
180	0	0
181	-0.0175	0.0349
182	-0.0349	0.0698
183	-0.0523	0.1045
184	-0.0698	0.1392
185	-0.0872	0.1736
186	-0.1045	0.2079
187	-0.1219	0.2419
188	-0.1392	0.2756
189	-0.1564	0.309
190	-0.1736	0.342
191	-0.1908	0.3746
192	-0.2079	0.4067
193	-0.225	0.4384
194	-0.2419	0.4695
195	-0.2588	0.5
196	-0.2756	0.5299
197	-0.2924	0.5592
198	-0.309	0.5878
199	-0.3256	0.6157
200	-0.342	0.6428
201	-0.3584	0.6691
202	-0.3746	0.6947
203	-0.3907	0.7193
204	-0.4067	0.7431
205	-0.4226	0.766
206	-0.4384	0.788
207	-0.454	0.809
208	-0.4695	0.829
209	-0.4848	0.848
210	-0.5	0.866
211	-0.515	0.8829
212	-0.5299	0.8988
213	-0.5446	0.9135
214	-0.5592	0.9272
215	-0.5736	0.9397

TABLE 9-2

CRANK ANGLE(α) [in Degrees]	c	d
216	-0.5878	0.9511
217	-0.6018	0.9613
218	-0.6157	0.9703
219	-0.6293	0.9781
220	-0.6428	0.9848
221	-0.6561	0.9903
222	-0.6691	0.9945
223	-0.682	0.9976
224	-0.6947	0.9994
225	-0.7071	1
226	-0.7193	0.9994
227	-0.7314	0.9976
228	-0.7431	0.9945
229	-0.7547	0.9903
230	-0.766	0.9848
231	-0.7771	0.9781
232	-0.788	0.9703
233	-0.7986	0.9613
234	-0.809	0.9511
235	-0.8192	0.9397
236	-0.829	0.9272
237	-0.8387	0.9135
238	-0.848	0.8988
239	-0.8572	0.8829
240	-0.866	0.866
241	-0.8746	0.848
242	-0.8829	0.829
243	-0.891	0.809
244	-0.8988	0.788
245	-0.9063	0.766
246	-0.9135	0.7431
247	-0.9205	0.7193
248	-0.9272	0.6947
249	-0.9336	0.6691
250	-0.9397	0.6428
251	-0.9455	0.6157

TABLE 9-2

CRANK ANGLE(α) [in Degrees]	c	d
252	-0.9511	0.5878
253	-0.9563	0.5592
254	-0.9613	0.5299
255	-0.9659	0.5
256	-0.9703	0.4695
257	-0.9744	0.4384
258	-0.9781	0.4067
259	-0.9816	0.3746
260	-0.9848	0.342
261	-0.9877	0.309
262	-0.9903	0.2756
263	-0.9925	0.2419
264	-0.9945	0.2079
265	-0.9962	0.1736
266	-0.9976	0.1392
267	-0.9986	0.1045
268	-0.9994	0.0698
269	-0.9998	0.0349
270	-1	0
271	-0.9998	-0.0349
272	-0.9994	-0.0698
273	-0.9986	-0.1045
274	-0.9976	-0.1392
275	-0.9962	-0.1736
276	-0.9945	-0.2079
277	-0.9925	-0.2419
278	-0.9903	-0.2756
279	-0.9877	-0.309
280	-0.9848	-0.342
281	-0.9816	-0.3746
282	-0.9781	-0.4067
283	-0.9744	-0.4384
284	-0.9703	-0.4695
285	-0.9659	-0.5
286	-0.9613	-0.5299
287	-0.9563	-0.5592

TABLE 9-2		
CRANK ANGLE(α) [in Degrees]	c	d
288	-0.9511	-0.5878
289	-0.9455	-0.6157
290	-0.9397	-0.6428
291	-0.9336	-0.6691
292	-0.9272	-0.6947
293	-0.9205	-0.7193
294	-0.9135	-0.7431
295	-0.9063	-0.766
296	-0.8988	-0.788
297	-0.891	-0.809
298	-0.8829	-0.829
299	-0.8746	-0.848
300	-0.866	-0.866
301	-0.8572	-0.8829
302	-0.848	-0.8988
303	-0.8387	-0.9135
304	-0.829	-0.9272
305	-0.8192	-0.9397
306	-0.809	-0.9511
307	-0.7986	-0.9613
308	-0.788	-0.9703
309	-0.7771	-0.9781
310	-0.766	-0.9848
311	-0.7547	-0.9903
312	-0.7431	-0.9945
313	-0.7314	-0.9976
314	-0.7193	-0.9994
315	-0.7071	-1
316	-0.6947	-0.9994
317	-0.682	-0.9976
318	-0.6691	-0.9945
319	-0.6561	-0.9903
320	-0.6428	-0.9848
321	-0.6293	-0.9781
322	-0.6157	-0.9703
323	-0.6018	-0.9613

TABLE 9-2		
CRANK ANGLE(α) [in Degrees]	c	d
324	-0.5878	-0.9511
325	-0.5736	-0.9397
326	-0.5592	-0.9272
327	-0.5446	-0.9135
328	-0.5299	-0.8988
329	-0.515	-0.8829
330	-0.5	-0.866
331	-0.4848	-0.848
332	-0.4695	-0.829
333	-0.454	-0.809
334	-0.4384	-0.788
335	-0.4226	-0.766
336	-0.4067	-0.7431
337	-0.3907	-0.7193
338	-0.3746	-0.6947
339	-0.3584	-0.6691
340	-0.342	-0.6428
341	-0.3256	-0.6157
342	-0.309	-0.5878
343	-0.2924	-0.5592
344	-0.2756	-0.5299
345	-0.2588	-0.5
346	-0.2419	-0.4695
347	-0.225	-0.4384
348	-0.2079	-0.4067
349	-0.1908	-0.3746
350	-0.1736	-0.342
351	-0.1564	-0.309
352	-0.1392	-0.2756
353	-0.1219	-0.2419
354	-0.1045	-0.2079
355	-0.0872	-0.1736
356	-0.0698	-0.1392
357	-0.0523	-0.1045
358	-0.0349	-0.0698
359	-0.0175	-0.0349

TABLE 9-2		
CRANK ANGLE(α) [in Degrees]	c	d
360	0	0

CHAPTER 10

STATIC COMPRESSION RATIO!

THIS OFTEN TALKED ABOUT, but frequently misunderstood entity, is a discrete constituent of engine performance. *It is defined as the ratio of the volume that is above the piston at bottom dead center to the volume that is above the piston at top dead center*, which also includes the combustion chamber and head gasket volumes whether the engine is in motion or not.

FREQUENTLY, MANY INDIVIDUALS TEND to compare engines based on this factor without taking into consideration the nature of the mass of air and fuel mixture entering the cylinder. Neither is the extent of fuel evaporation or saturation of the cylinder by this mixture, ring seal, valve seating and type of fuel being used, given careful consideration. Although, when closely evaluated, these factors can yield a better perspective of the potential that's offered by the static compression ratio. Simply stated, the lesser the quantity of air-fuel mixture drawn into(that is to be compressed) or inducted into the cylinder, and the greater the reduction in saturation thereof, the engine's optimum power potential will be restricted, regardless of the compression ratio! Notwithstanding, the more air and fuel delivered to the cylinders, and the greater the saturation of the mixture--not excluding piston ring seal, proper valve seating,etc.--the engine will possess the potential to develop more power. Also, note that it is possible for an engine to have a smaller compression ratio than another engine, and produce more torque and horsepower because of an improved air-fuel mixture(better saturation of the mixture per cylinder). This takes in consideration that some factors will be equal. In addition, this can be attained quite possibly while consuming a smaller quantity of air and fuel.

TO CALCULATE THE STATIC COMPRESSION ratio such things as the combustion chamber, gasket, deck height clearance, piston dome, and cylinder volumes for a single cylinder must be known. **The basic equation for this ratio is...**

$$\text{Static C. R.} = \frac{(ccv + hgv + pdv + dcv + sv)}{(ccv + hgv + pdv + dcv)}$$

Where,

Static C.R. -- is the static compression ratio
ccv -- is the combustion chamber volume per cylinder, in cubic centermeters(cc)
hgv -- is the compressed head gasket volume per cylinder(cc)
pdv -- is the piston dome or dish volume per cylinder(cc)
dcv -- is the deck height clearance volume per cylinder(cc)
sv -- is the swept volume resulting from the piston moving from TDC-to-BDC or from BDC-to-TDC

IT IS IMPORTANT TO NOTE THE FOLLOWING:

- If the piston has a dome or a protrusion, its volume is considered to be negative(-) because this reduces the combustion chamber volume(-pdv).

- If the piston is dished, concave, or has valve reliefs on top, its volume will be considered as positive(+) because it increases the effective clearance volume(+pdv). In like manner, this applies to any notches, grooves, impressions, or designs made in the piston's crown.

- If the piston has a flat top with no alterations to its crown, the cylinder head's combustion chamber volume will then be unaffected.

FIGURE 10-1 SHOWS THE basic piston configurations. Other examples are in the following figures.

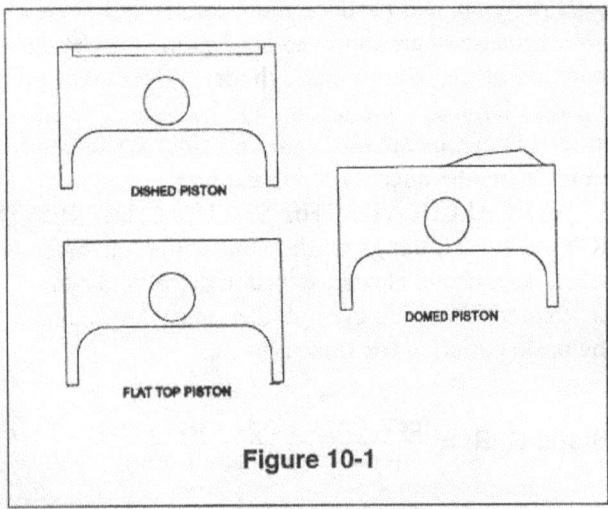

Figure 10-1

Figure 10-2: The two pistons shown above are dished pistons with valve reliefs for the intake and exhaust valves.
Photographs -- Courtesy of GM Performance Parts

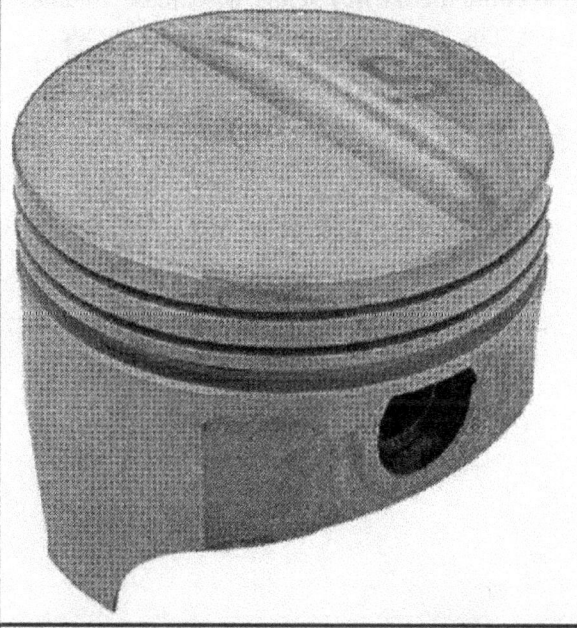

Figure 10-3: Shown above are two types of flat top pistons with valve reliefs for the intake and exhaust valves.
Photographs -- Courtesy of GM Performance Parts

THREE ANALYTICAL OR MATHEMATICAL SOLUTIONS ARE given to expound on this matter. They are, (1) a dished, concaved, or flat top piston with any alterations in its crown, (2) a flat top piston with no alterations to its crown, and (3) a domed piston.

Figure 10-4: Shown above is a domed piston with valve reliefs for the intake and exhaust valves.
Photograph -- Courtesy of GM Performance Parts

Case-1
For a dished, concaved, or flat top piston with any alterations in its crown, the static compression ratio can be calculated from the following equation.

$$\text{Static C. R.}(1) = 1 + \frac{sv}{(ccv + hgv + pdv + dcv)}$$

Case-2
For a flat top piston with no alterations to its crown (no valve reliefs, etc.), the compression ratio is given by the following equation.

$$\text{Static C. R.}(2) = 1 + \frac{sv}{(ccv + hgv + dcv)}$$

Case-3
For a domed piston, the compression ratio is given by the following equation.

$$\text{Static C. R.}(3) = 1 + \frac{sv}{(ccv + hgv - pdv + dcv)}$$

EXAMPLE(10a):
The following engine parameters are given for "Case-1", and the static compression ratio will be...

sv = 783.3 cc
ccv = 60 cubic centimeters(cc)
hgv = 9.7 cc(for a 4.00" bore, and .047" thickness.)
pdv = 10 cc
dcv = 3.5 cc(for a 4.00" bore, and .017" ht.)

$$\text{Static C. R.}(1) = 1 + \frac{sv}{(ccv + hgv + pdv + dcv)}$$

$$\text{Static C. R.}(1) = 1 + \frac{783.3}{(60 + 9.7 + 10 + 3.5)}$$

$$\text{Static C. R.}(1) = 1 + \frac{783.3}{83.2}$$

Static C. R.(1) = 1 + 9.41

Static C. R.(1) = 10.41

EXAMPLE(10b):
Using the same engine parameters from EXAMPLE(10-1) for "Case-2", the static compression ratio will be...

$$\text{Static C. R.}(2) = 1 + \frac{sv}{(ccv + hgv + dcv)}$$

$$\text{Static C. R.}(2) = 1 + \frac{783.3}{(60 + 9.7 + 3.5)}$$

$$\text{Static C. R.}(2) = 1 + \frac{783.3}{73.2}$$

Static C. R.(2) = 1 + 10.70

Static C. R.(2) = 11.70

EXAMPLE(10c): Using the same engine parameters from EXAMPLE(10a) for "Case-3", the static compression ratio will be...

$$\text{Static C. R.}(3) = 1 + \frac{sv}{(ccv + hgv - pdv + dcv)}$$

$$\text{Static C. R.}(3) = 1 + \frac{783.3}{(60 + 9.7 - 10 + 3.5)}$$

$$\text{Static C. R.}(3) = 1 + \frac{783.3}{63.2}$$

Static C. R.(3) = 1 + 12.39

Static C. R.(3) = 13.39

THE UNITS WERE given in -- **cc's** --for computing the static compression ratios in the previous examples. They can also be calculated in **cubic inches** using the conversion factor of **1 cubic inch = 16.387 cc**, provided that the engine's cylinder volume is given in **cubic inches(in^3)**. Otherwise, these volumes will have to be measured using a graduated burette.

CHAPTER 11

Dynamic Compression Ratio!!!

UNLIKE THE STATIC COMPRESSION RATIO which is a ratio of two volumes - when the piston is at both bottom dead center and top dead center -- *the dynamic compression ratio, as it will be called, is a function of 1) valve timing, and 2) when the piston is at TDC.* This means that during the compression process or stroke the theoretical compression of the air-fuel mixture begins to take place at the point or time when the intake valve is fully closed(see Figure 11-1). Consequently, beginning at such a point, the dynamic swept volume **-- the volume above the piston at the point when the intake valve has completely closed, minus the volume above the piston when it is at TDC --** can be calculated, along with the usual combustion chamber calculations.

BEFORE WE EXPLORE the method of calculating this ratio, it is essential to observe the effects of this process. Depending on the valves overlap period(the phase when the intake and exhaust valves are open together or at the same time), the intake valve opening time, the incoming mixture temperature, ambient conditions, cubic inch displacement, static compression ratio, intake valve and exhaust valve sizes, carburetor, intake and exhaust manifolding, the mixture's flow rate(the amount of air and fuel entering the engine over a specified period of time) of the air and fuel entering the cylinders can only reach a specific value for a particular engine speed. With this in mind, it is important to understand that changing the valve timing by changing the camshaft, or adjusting the rockers(for a non-hydraulic lifter cam) will change the dynamic compression ratio, & ultimately the mass flow rate. Also, keep in mind that if there are reductions in the quantity of air and fuel entering the cylinders, the engine's power may be stunted irrespectful of the dynamic compression ratio's value!

NOW TO EXPLORE THE method of calculating this ratio. It is somewhat different from the static

> ...during the compression process or stroke the theoretical compression of the air-fuel mixture begins to take place at the point or time when the intake valve is fully closed.

compression ratio in that it is a function of the number of degrees of crankshaft rotation, stroke, throw, and connecting rod length.

The basic equation for the "Dynamic Compression Ratio"(Dynamic C.R.) is...

$$\text{Dynamic C. R.} = \frac{(ccv + hgv + pdv + dcv + dsv)}{(ccv + hgv + pdv + dcv)}$$

Dynamic C.R. -- is the dynamic compression ratio

ccv -- is the combustion chamber volume per cylinder, in cubic centermeters(cc)

hgv -- is the compressed head gasket volume per cylinder(cc)

pdv -- is the piston dome or dish volume per cylinder(cc)

dcv -- is the deck height clearance volume per cylinder(cc)

dsv -- is the dynamic swept volume; this is the volume remaining above the piston after the piston has moved from BDC to some point or angle ABDC

THREE ANALYTICAL OR MATHEMATICAL SOLUTIONS ARE given to expound on this matter. They are, (1) a dished, concaved, or flat top piston with any alterations in its crown, (2) a flat top piston with no alterations to its crown, and (3) a domed piston.

Case-1
For a dished, concaved, or flat top piston with any alterations in its crown, the static compression ratio can be calculated from the following equation(see Figure 10-1, Figure 10-2, and Figure 10-3).

$$\text{Dynamic C. R.(1)} = 1 + \frac{dsv}{(ccv + hgv + pdv + dcv)}$$

Case-2
For a flat top piston with no alterations to its crown(no valve reliefs, etc.), the compression ratio is given by the following equation(see Figure 10-1).

$$\text{Dynamic C. R.(2)} = 1 + \frac{dsv}{(ccv + hgv + dcv)}$$

Case-3
For a domed piston, the compression ratio is given by the following equation(see Figure 10-1, and Figure 10-4).

$$\text{Dynamic C. R.(3)} = 1 + \frac{dsv}{(ccv + hgv - pdv + dcv)}$$

EXAMPLE(11):
During the compression stroke of a spark ignition engine -- with flat top pistons having no alterations to their crown's -- the intake valve closes at $62°$ ABDC, the dynamic compression ratio for the following data will be...

Given:
1) ccv= 60 cc, dcv = 3.5 cc, and hgv = 9.7 cc
2) a cylinder bore of 4.00 in
3) a stroke equal to 3.25 in
4) and a connecting rod length of 5.70 in

If the dynamic compression ratio were to be calculated using cubic inches, the ccv, hgv, dcv, and pdv would need to be converted from cubic centimeters(cc).
Since there are 16.387 cc's per cubic inch(16.387 cc/in^3), this implies that...

$$60 \text{ cc} = 60 \text{ cc} / (16.387 \text{ cc}/in^3) = 3.661 \text{ in}^3$$

- now -

$$\text{Cylinder Area} = 0.7854 \times \text{Bore} \times \text{Bore}$$

Cylinder Area = 0.7854 x 4 in x 4 in

Cylinder Area = 0.7854 x 16 in^2

Cylinder Area = 12.5663 in^2

Next, the crank throw must be known, so...

Crank Throw = stroke/2 = 3.25 in/2 = 1.625 in

Finally, the piston travel must be determined from the following equation:

$$PD = \text{Crank Throw} \times \left[(1 - a) + \frac{\text{Crank Throw}}{2 \times \text{Rod length}} \times b\right]$$

Where,

- PD -- is the piston displacement calculated in inches(in)
- Crank Throw -- is the crankshaft's radius of rotation given in inches
- Rod Length -- is the connecting rod length given in inches(in)
- a -- is the cos(pronounced -- cosine) of the crank angle(α) and is given in Table 6-1
- b -- is the sin(pronounced -- sine) of the crank angle(α) times itself[i.e. - sin(α) x sin(α)] and is given in Table 6-1
- α -- is the crank angle measured clockwise in degrees(°)

For a given timing of 62° ABDC(see Figure 11-1, page 68), this means the crankshaft first rotates thru 180 degrees -- one-half revolution -- and through an additional 62 degrees). Therefore, the crank angle(α) is equal to the sum of these two values.

α = 180° + 62° = 242° ↓(+),

[The arrow denotes clockwise(cw) rotation of the crank, which will be considered as positive. Note the plus sign.]

- also -

An equivalent value for the crank angle(α) of rotation can be obtained by using a counter clockwise(ccw) rotation of the crankshaft[which is negative(-)] thereby subtracting 360°(one full revolution of the crankshaft) from 242°.

α = 242° - 360° = - 118° ↑(-)

[The arrows denote a counter clockwise rotation, which is negative.]

So,

For a crank angle(α) of 242°(ATDC) from Table 6-1; <u>a</u> is equal to <u>-0.4695</u>, and <u>b</u> is equal to <u>0.7796</u>.

$$PD = \text{Crank Throw} \times \left[(1 - a) + \frac{\text{Crank Throw}}{2 \times \text{Rod length}} \times b\right]$$

PD = 1.625 in x (1 - (-0.4695) + $\frac{1.625 \text{ in}}{2 \times 5.70 \text{ in}}$ x 0.7796)

PD = 1.625 in x (1 + 0.4695) + $\frac{1.625}{11.4}$ x 0.7796)

PD = 1.625 in x (1.4695 + 0.1425 x 0.7796)

PD = 1.625 in x (1.4695 + 0.1111)

PD = 1.625 in x (1.5806)

PD = 2.5685 in

THIS SAY'S THAT THE top of the piston is at a location that is **2.5685 inches** down **from top dead center(TDC)**.

IF THE VALUES FOR <u>a</u> and <u>b</u> are inserted into the equation from **Table 6-1** for the **118°** crank angle, you will see that they will yield the same answer!

NOW, SINCE THE **cylinder area** and **piston travel** are known, the "**dynamic swept volume**" can be calculated as follows:

dsv -- **dynamic swept volume**

dsv = Cylinder Area x PD

dsv = 12.5663 in² x 2.5685 in

dsv = 32.2765 in³(cubic inches)

- also -

dsv = 32.2765 in³ x 16.387 cc/in³ = 528.915 cc

CHAPTER ELEVEN

Now using the equation for "Case-2", and for ccv = 60 cc, dcv = 3.5 cc, and hgv = 9.7 cc, the dynamic compression ratio is...

$$\text{Dynamic C. R.}(2) = 1 + \frac{dsv}{(ccv + hgv + dcv)}$$

$$\text{Dynamic C. R.}(2) = 1 + \frac{528.915 \text{ cc}}{(60 \text{ cc} + 9.7 \text{ cc} + 3.5 \text{ cc})}$$

$$\text{Dynamic C. R.}(2) = 1 + \frac{528.915 \text{ cc}}{73.2 \text{ cc}}$$

$$\text{Dynamic C. R.}(2) = 1 + 7.226$$

$$\text{Dynamic C. R.}(2) = 8.226$$

Compare this number to that of the "static compression ratios" computation utilizing the same type of piston. You can see the **Dynamic C.R.(Dynamic Compression Ratio)** is less than the **Static C.R.(Static Compression Ratio)**, and will most likely always be less.

You may wonder what significance this is, if any. Well, there is a significance, and that is in general, *the lower the D.C.R., the higher the static compression ratio can be for a normally aspirated engine.* However, fuel octane, air-fuel ratio, air-fuel mixture intake valve timing, ignition timing, valve overlap, and combustion chamber design are major factors that can have an influence on the maximum practical value for the **C.R.**

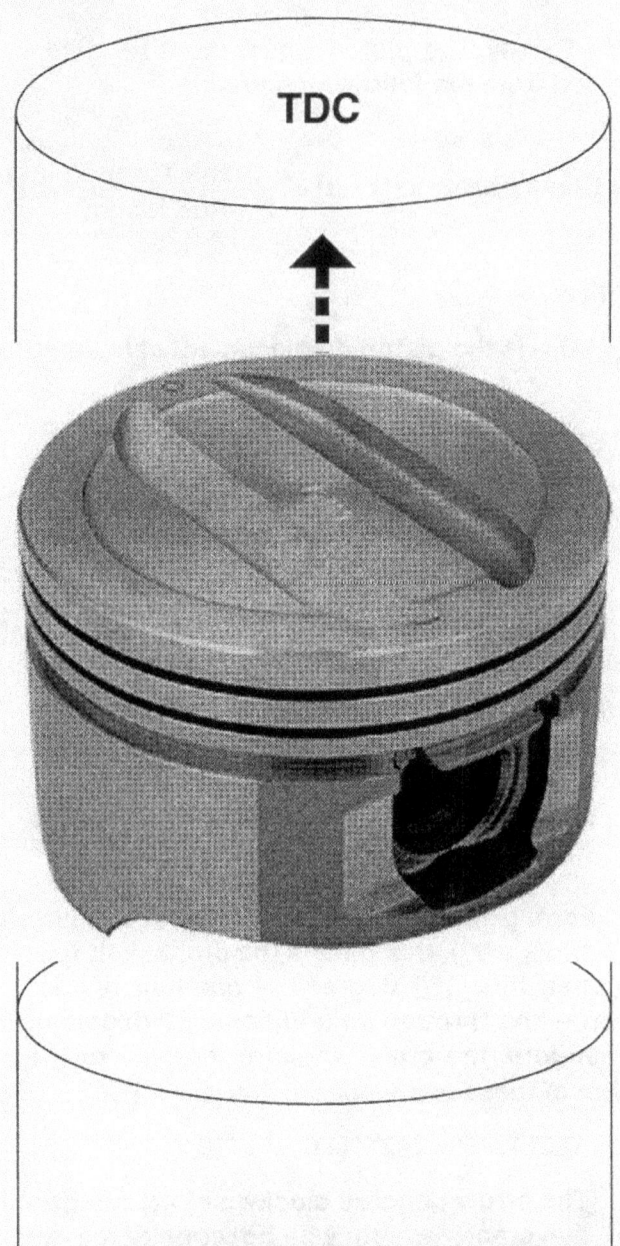

Figure 11-1: This illustration shows the location of the piston at some point or crank angle in the cylinder bore after moving up from BDC toward TDC.
Photo -- Courtesy of GM Performance Parts

CHAPTER 12

AIR MASS
EFFICIENCY!

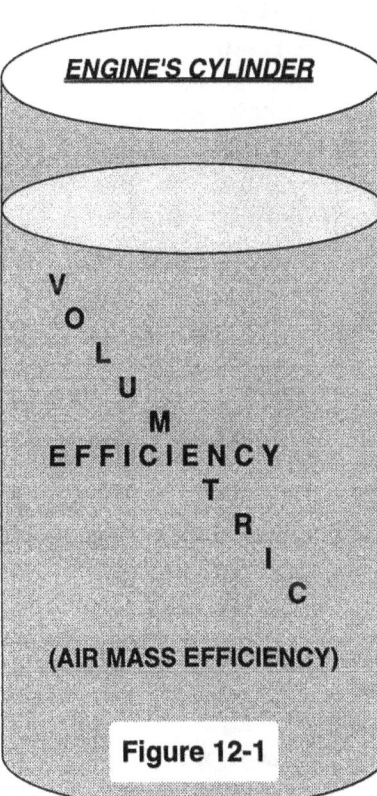

Figure 12-1

ENGINE PERFORMANCE IS directly related to the masses of air that enters the cylinders. The greater the quantity of air mass, the higher will be the cylinder's peak pressure during the compression and combustion processes for any air-fuel ratio. This will ultimately increase the torque output with a corresponding increase in horsepower. The air mass charge (the amount of inducted air) that goes into the engine's cylinders (see Figure 12-1) is dictated by the efficiency of the engine's intake system, exhaust system, valve timing, and engine speed.

THIS BRINGS US to the so called expression, *"volumetric efficiency"*, *which will be referred to as the "air mass efficiency". It is defined as the ratio of the actual mass of air taken into the cylinder in relation to the theoretical mass of air that could be taken into the cylinder.*

THE EQUATION FOR THE *air mass efficiency* is...

$$\text{Air Mass Eff} = \frac{\text{Actual mass of air}}{\text{Theoretical mass of air}}$$

Where,

Air Mass Eff -- is the "Air Mass Efficiency"

Actual mass of air -- is the actual mass of air taken into the cylinder under atmospheric or prescribed test conditions

Theoretical mass of air -- is the theoretical mass of air that could be taken into the cylinder under atmospheric or prescribed test conditions

THE EXPRESSION "volumetric efficiency" may not be suitable, because, actually this is a "mass ratio", and not a "volume ratio". This ratio could very well be called the cylinder's *"air mass ratio"*. This efficiency is also affected by the method with which the air and fuel are inducted or either the fuel is induced into the engine, when using carburetors or fuel injection, respectively. The shapes and sizes of the combustion chamber, pistons, intake and exhaust ports will affect the cylinder(s) filling potential also. *From here on end in this book, it(vol. efficiency) will be referred to as the engine's "air mass efficiency".*

IN CONJUNCTION, any obstruction along the path(s) of air flow, including port roughness, generates pressure waves that move opposite to the direction of flow through the medium(air). This occurs at a speed relative to its elasticity and density. These waves travel back to the inlet of the intake system where atmospheric pressure exists, and signals the incoming air to move at a velocity proportional to them.

DURING IDLE -- WHEN THE throttle plates are almost closed -- the ambient(atmospheric) pressure above or ahead of the throttle plates is greater than the pressure below or behind it(vacuum). At this point the air velocity is at a minimum because of the impediments resulting from the throttle plates, venturi boosters, and choke plate, if any. These elements cause strong pressure waves to be produced, that result from the build up of air in front of the throttle plates. These pressure waves are continuously reflected back through the air until all the incoming air is able to sense the obstruction, and thus, maintaining a low air velocity.

AT WIDE OPEN THROTTLE, THE pressure difference throughout the intake system is at its least value and there is minimal impedance to the air flow. This yields weaker pressure waves that signal the oncoming air of the lower resistance, and therefore causes an increase in the flow rate of air into the cylinder(s).

IN THE REAL WORLD, the air is not pure; it is mixed with water-vapor and other elements making up our atmosphere. *The atmosphere is a gaseous mass that surrounds the earth. This gaseous mass is made primarily of air and water-vapor. The ratio of the partial pressure of the water-vapor, in a mixture of air & water-vapor, to the saturation pressure of water at the same dry bulb temperature is defined as the relative humidity.* The terms *partial pressure, saturation pressure, and dry bulb temperature* are defined as follows:

- **PARTIAL PRESSURE -- The pressure that is exerted by an element in a mixture such as air, or <u>water-vapor</u> in an air and <u>water-vapor</u> mixture.**
- **SATURATION PRESSURE -- The pressure at which vaporization of a liquid takes place at a given temperature.**
- **DRY BULB TEMPERATURE -- The actual atmospheric(whether indoors or out-of-doors) temperature measurement as indicated by a plain graduated thermometer.**

THE RELATIVE HUMIDITY plays a significant part in an engine's performance, since it affects the rate of combustion of the air-fuel mixture and air mass ratio efficiency due to the mass of water-vapor.

An example of water-vapor in the atmosphere is revealed in the subsequent calculations.

EXAMPLE(12):
For a 350 cubic inch eight(8) cylinder engine operating at 6000 rpm in an atmospheric pressure(barometric pressure) of 30.10 in-Hg, an atmospheric temperature of 80°F, and 75% relative humidity at wide open throttle; the (a) theoretical mass of air per cylinder, (b) the actual mass of air per cylinder, (c) the air mass efficiency, (d) the reduction in the air mass efficiency due to the humidity, (e) and the net air mass efficiency will be...

EXAMPLE(12a): The theoretical mass of air per cylinder is...

$$\text{Theo Air Mass} = \frac{\text{Atm Pressure} \times \text{Cyl Volume} \times .083 \text{ ft/in}}{53.34 \text{ ft-lbf/lbm-}°R \times \text{Atm Temp}}$$

Where,

Actual Air Mass -- actual mass of air
Theo Air Mass -- theoretical mass of air
Atm Pres -- Atmospheric Pressure(lbf/in^2)
Baro Pres -- Barometric Pressure
Baro Pres -- Atmospheric Pressure(in-hg)

Cyl Volume -- Cylinder Volume(in^3)
Gas Constant for Air -- 53.34 ft-lbf/lbm-^{0}R
Atm Temp -- Atmospheric Temperature(^{0}R)
^{0}R -- Degrees Rankine
^{0}R -- ^{0}F + 459.67

Since the **atmospheric pressure and temperature** are given in **inches of mercury and degrees Fahrenheit**, it will be necessary to convert both values to the proper units in order to complete the calculations for the actual and theoretical air masses.

Hence,

Atm Pres = baro pres x (0.491 lbf/in^2/(in-hg))
Atm Pres = 30.10 in-hg x (0.491 lbf/in^2/(in-hg))
Atm Pres = 14.7791 lbf/in^2

And,

Atm Temp = ^{0}F + 459.67
Atm Temp = 80^0F + 459.67
Atm Temp = 539.67^0R

Also,

$$\text{Volume per Cylinder} = \frac{\text{Engine Displ}}{\text{No. Cylinders}}$$

$$\text{Volume per Cylinder} = \frac{350 \text{ in}^3}{8 \text{ Cylinders}}$$

Volume per Cylinder = 43.75 in^3 / Cyl

Now,

$$\text{Theo Air Mass} = \frac{\text{Atm Pres x Cyl Volume x .083 ft/in}}{53.34 \text{ ft-lbf/lbm-}^0\text{R x Atm Temp}}$$

$$\text{Theo Air Mass} = \frac{14.779 \text{ lbf/in}^2 \text{ x } 43.75 \text{ in}^3 \text{ x } .083 \text{ ft/in}}{53.34 \text{ ft-lbf/lbm-}^0\text{R x } 539.67 \text{ }^0\text{R}}$$

$$\text{Theo Air Mass} = \frac{53.6662 \text{ lbf-ft}}{28785.9978 \text{ ft-lbf/lbm}}$$

Theo Air Mass = 0.00186432 lbm

EXAMPLE(12b): The actual mass of air is...

$$\text{Act Air Mass} = \frac{\text{AP x Cyl Volume x .083 ft/in}}{53.34 \text{ ft-lbf/lbm-}^0\text{R x Atm Temp}}$$

Act Air Mass -- Actual Air Mass per cylinder
AP -- Partial air pressure
VP -- Partial vapor pressure

As stated before, the air is composed of water-vapor and is not pure. In reality the **air** and **water-vapor** each exert a certain amount of pressure in the atmosphere. These pressures are called "**partial pressures**".

Therefore,

Atm Pres -- is the partial pressure of the air exerted in the mixture of air & <u>water-vapor</u> + the partial pressure of the <u>water-vapor</u> exerted in a mixture of air & <u>water-vapor</u>(vapor pressure)

Atm Pres = AP + VP

Solving for **AP** yields...

AP = Atm Pres - VP

Since the "**relative humidity**" is given, and is a function of the **vapor pressure(VP)**, it stands that...

relative humidity = VP / GP = 75% / 100 = .75

GP -- is the saturation pressure of the water-vapor @ the same temperature as for VP ...

The value of **GP** can be acquired from a thermodynamic steam table or from the enclosed **thermodynamic steam table data in Table 12-1** at the end of this chapter.

@ 80^0F, GP = .50683 lbf/in^2

For: VP / GP = .75
VP = .75 x GP = .75 x .50683 lbf/in^2
VP = .3801 lbf/in^2

AP = Atm Pres - VP

AP = 14.779 lbf/in² - .3081 lbf/in²

AP = 14.4709 lbf/in²

So,

$$\text{Act Air Mass} = \frac{\text{AP} \times \text{Cyl Volume} \times .083 \text{ ft/in}}{53.34 \text{ ft-lbf/lbm-}°\text{R} \times \text{Atm Temp}}$$

$$\text{Act Air Mass} = \frac{14.4709 \text{ lbf/in}^2 \times 43.75 \text{ in}^3 \times .083 \text{ ft/in}}{53.34 \text{ ft-lbf/lbm-}°\text{R} \times 539.67°\text{R}}$$

$$\text{Act Air Mass} = \frac{52.5475 \text{ lbf-ft}}{28785.9978 \text{ ft-lbf/lbm}}$$

Act Air Mass = .00182545 lbm

EXAMPLE(12c): The Air Mass Efficiency is...

$$\text{Air Mass Eff} = \frac{\text{Actual mass of air}}{\text{Theoretical mass of air}}$$

$$\text{Air Mass Eff} = \frac{.00182545 \text{ lbm}}{.00186432 \text{ lbm}}$$

Air Mass Eff = 0.97915058

- And -

% Air Mass Eff = 0.97915058 x 100

% Air Mass Eff = 97.915058%

- Rounded Off -

% Air Mass Eff = 97.92%

EXAMPLE(12d): The percent reduction in air mass efficiency is...

Air Mass Eff(% reduc) = 100% - Air Mass Eff

Air Mass Eff(% reduc) = 100% - 97.92%

Air Mass Eff(% reduc) = 2.08 %

- or the decimal equivalent is -

Air Mass Eff(reduc) = 1 - .97915058

Air Mass Eff(reduc) = .02084942

THIS SECTION DEALS WITH THE "Net Air Mass Efficiency".

THE NET AIR MASS efficiency is determined by including the air mass efficiency as a function of the engine speed.

THE EQUATIONS ARE as follows:

Air Mass Eff(Carb) -- Air mass efficiency based on the carburetors air flow rate

Air Mass Eff(rpm) -- Air mass efficiency based on the carburetor's or intake manifold's rpm rating

AME -- Air mass efficiency
Cfm -- Carburetor air flow capacity
Cu in -- Engine displacement
rpm -- Engine speed

- If the carburetor's <u>rated</u> flow rate is used, then...

$$\text{Air Mass Eff(Carb)} = \frac{\text{Cu in} \times \text{Engine rpm}}{\text{Carburetor cfm} \times 3456}$$

- *If an engine's cubic inch displacement is assumed constant(w/the carburetor being flow rated for this engine displacement), the air mass efficiency is then largely a function of the maximum engine speed, and a function of the carburetor's or intake manifold's maximum rpm rating as shown below.*

$$\text{Air Mass Eff(rpm)} = \frac{\text{Carb or Intake rpm}}{\text{Engine rpm}}$$

Net AME(carb) = Air Mass Eff(Carb) - (1 - AME)

- or -

Net AME(rpm) = Air Mass Eff(rpm) - (1 - AME)

Net AME(carb)Cfm -- Net air mass efficiency as a result of "Air Mass Eff(Carb)"

Net AME(rpm) -- Net air mass efficiency as a result of "Air Mass Eff(rpm)"

EXAMPLE(12e): The net air mass efficiency is...

(1) For the previous mentioned engine speed of 6000 rpm and a <u>rated</u> carburetor cfm of 600.

$$\text{Air Mass Eff(Carb)} = \frac{\text{Carburetor cfm} \times 3456}{\text{Cu in} \times \text{Engine rpm}}$$

$$\text{Air Mass Eff(Carb)} = \frac{600 \text{ ft}^3/\text{min} \times 3456 \text{ in}^3/\text{ft}^3}{350 \text{ in}^3 \times 6000 \text{ rev/min}}$$

$$\text{Air Mass Eff(Carb)} = \frac{2073600 \text{ in}^3/\text{min}}{2100000 \text{ in}^3/\text{min}}$$

Air Mass Eff(Carb) = 0.98742857

Therefore,

Net AME(carb) = Air Mass Eff(Carb) - (1 - AME)

Net AME(carb) = 0.98742857 - (1 - 0.97915058)

Net AME(carb) = 0.98742857 - 0.02084942

Net AME(carb) = 0.96657915

(Rounded off, the maximum theoretical air mass efficiency is therefore <u>.9612</u> or <u>96.12%</u>.)

---

(2) If a carburetor's cubic inch displacement rating and engine's cubic inch displacement are the same, and the carburetor's flow rate peaks at 5500 rpm while the engine operates at a maximum speed of 6000, then...

$$\text{Air Mass Eff(rpm)} = \frac{\text{Carb or Intake rpm}}{\text{Engine rpm}}$$

$$\text{Air Mass Eff(rpm)} = \frac{5500 \text{ rpm}}{6000 \text{ rpm}}$$

Air Mass Eff(rpm) = 0.91666667

Therefore,

Net AME(rpm) = Air Mass Eff(rpm) - (1 - AME)

Net AME(rpm) = 0.91666667 - (1 - 0.97915058)

Net AME(rpm) = 0.91666667 - 0.02084942

Net AME(rpm) = 0.89581725

(Rounded off, the maximum theoretical air mass efficiency is therefore <u>.8904</u> or <u>89.04%</u>.)

All temperature and pressure data given on the following page in Table 12-1 is printed by permission of the ASME; from Table <u>1</u> of the 1983, 5th edition, of the saturated steam and saturated water(temperature) tables.

- The temperature is given in degrees fahrenheit(^{0}F)
- The unit of pressure is expressed in psia -- pounds per square inch, absolute(lb/in^2)

CHAPTER TWELVE

TABLE 12-1
[SATURATION TEMPERATURES AND PRESSURES]

Temperature °F	Pressure (psia-lb/in²)	Temperature °F	Pressure (psia-lb/in²)	Temperature °F	Pressure (psia-lb/in²)
32	0.08859	62	0.27494	93	0.76655
32.018	0.08865	63	0.2848	94	0.79062
33	0.09223	64	0.29497	95	0.81534
34	0.096	65	0.30545	96	0.84072
35	0.09991	66	0.31626	97	0.86679
36	0.10395	67	0.3274	98	0.89356
37	0.10815	68	0.33889	99	0.92103
38	0.11249	69	0.35073	100	0.94924
39	0.11698	70	0.36292	101	0.97818
40	0.12163	71	0.37549	102	1.00789
41	0.12645	72	0.38844	103	1.03838
42	0.13143	73	0.40177	104	1.06965
43	0.13659	74	0.4155	105	1.10174
44	0.14192	75	0.42964	106	1.1347
45	0.14744	76	0.4442	107	1.1684
46	0.15314	77	0.45919	108	1.203
47	0.15904	78	0.47461	109	1.2385
48	0.16514	79	0.49049	110	1.275
49	0.17144	80	0.50683	111	1.3123
50	0.17796	81	0.52364	112	1.3505
51	0.18469	82	0.54093	113	1.3898
52	0.19165	83	0.55872	114	1.4299
53	0.19883	84	0.57702	115	1.4711
54	0.20625	85	0.59583	116	1.5133
55	0.21392	86	0.61518	117	1.5566
56	0.22183	87	0.63507	118	1.6009
57	0.23	88	0.65551	119	1.6463
58	0.23843	89	0.67653	120	1.6927
59	0.24713	90	0.69813		
60	0.25611	91	0.72032		
61	0.26538	92	0.74313		

CHAPTER 13

BRAKE MEAN EFFECTIVE PRESSURE (BMEP)

OF THE FOUR strokes -- the intake, compression, expansion -or- power, and exhaust -- which comprise a full cycle of operation in the spark ignition, gasoline driven, internal combustion engine; the power stroke is the main positive influence that contributes to the work output. The three remaining strokes are principally negative due to the pumping losses throughout the intake and exhaust strokes, and compression of the air-fuel mixture(see Figure 13-1). This means they absorb power from the engine, or

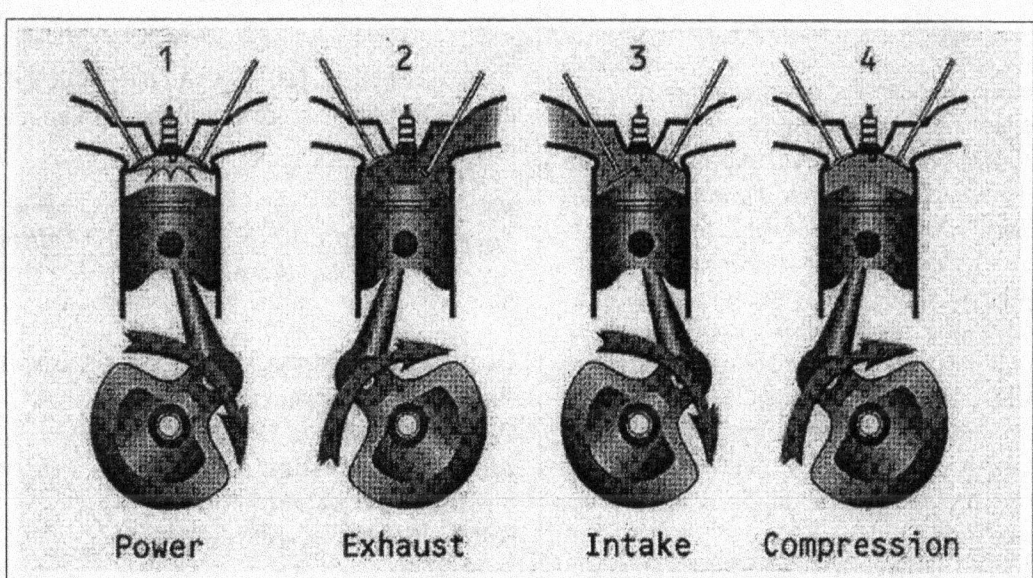

Figure 13-1: (1) Ignition of the air-fuel mixture takes place; (2) The burnt air-fuel mixture is expelled from the cylinder; (3) Fresh air-fuel mixture charge is drawn into the cylinder; (4) Compression of the air fuel mixture takes place.
Illustration -- Reproduced by permission of COMP Cams®

work contrary to it to some degree. DURING THE expansion -or- power stroke, the pressure in the cylinder(s) does not remain constant throughout the entire stroke. Instead, it continuously decreases as the piston moves away from top dead center until the exhaust valve opens before the piston reaches bottom dead center. Once the exhaust valve opens, the remaining pressure in the cylinder is suddenly released, and the pressure in the cylinder decreases close to atmospheric. It should be noted that the pressure decreases in the cylinder during the power stroke, and the rate at which the pressure declines is not linear. It would be very cumbersome in making an effort to manually calculate any engine's overall or total work(torque) and power output for each degree of crankshaft rotation. This is because there is a corresponding change in cylinder volume and cylinder pressure that subsist, with a consequent change in the combustion temperature for this non-linear relation-

> "...torque is not a good indicator of performance alone..."
>
> "Engines should neither be compared on the basis of their horsepower output <u>alone</u>..."

ship. Therefore, a means is necessitous in order to simplify this method for aiding in determining the engine's output. This means will also be used to compare dissimilar engines; *it is called the* **mean effective pressure(MEP)**. THE *MEP* IS THAT constant pressure that can be thought of or envisioned to be applied during the duration of the power stroke(until the exhaust valve opens), whether it is an indicated mean effective pressure(IMEP) or brake mean effective pressure(BMEP). It can be said that it is the average of all the pressures exerted per degree of crankshaft rotation during the power stroke, minus the averages of the negative pressures of the intake, compression, and exhaust strokes.

BEFORE DEFINING THE LAST two pressures let us focus first on the previous statement by which the mean effective pressure will also be used to compare various engines. What this means for example is that torque is not a good indicator of performance alone since it depends greatly on the engine's size; most likely, the larger cubic inch engine will produce the most torque. Engines should neither be compared solely on their horsepower output alone, because, horsepower is a function of cubic inch displacement and engine speed. Consequently, the engine with the greatest cubic inch displacement and rpm limit, possesses the greatest possibility of developing the most power. This can also apply when the engine's cubic inch displacements are the same.

ON THE CONTRARY THE MEP is the factor that reveals how the engine's displacement is utilized in helping to generate torque or work at the crankshaft. Stated otherwise, the product of the mean effective pressure and the engine displacement yields the work output of the engine.

NOW TO DEFINE THE *IMEP* AND *BMEP*.

- IMEP(Indicated Mean effective Pressure) -- is that theoretical constant pressure that can be thought of or envisioned to be applied during the duration of the power stroke, until the exhaust valve opens.

- BMEP(Brake Mean Effective Pressure) -- is the IMEP minus the FMEP(Friction MEP), which is the amount of mean effective pressure that is necessary to overcome friction in the engine.

- BMEP = IMEP - FMEP

THEREFORE, THE EQUATION FOR THE brake mean effective pressure as a function of engine horsepower is...

$$BMEP = \frac{Bhp \times 12 \text{ in/ft} \times 33000 \text{ ft-lbf/min} \times Z}{Cyl\ Area \times Stroke \times n \times RPM}$$

BMEP - Brake Mean Effective Pressure(lbf/in^2)
Bhp -- Brake horsepower
Cyl Area -- area of the cylinder(in^2)
Stroke -- crankshaft stroke(in)
n -- the number of cylinders
RPM -- Engine speed(rev/min)

Z -- the number of revolutions necessary to to accomplish one power stroke per piston
- (Z = 1, for a two stroke engine)
- (Z = 2, for a four stroke engine)

EXAMPLE(13):
Now, let's assume that you have or want to build an eight cylinder, four(4) stroke, 400 horsepower engine. Let your engine have a cylinder bore that is 4.125" in diameter, with a 3.50" stroke, and a peak crankshaft speed of 7000 rpm. Determine the amount of brake mean effective pressure(bmep) that is necessary to generate this amount of horsepower.

From the given information, the piston or cylinder area(Cyl Area) perpendicular to the centerline of the cylinder(s) must be known.

So,

Cyl Area = 0.7854 x Bore x Bore
Cyl Area = 0.7854 x 4.125 in x 4.125 in
Cyl Area = 0.7854 x 17.0156 in^2
Cyl Area = 13.3641 in^2

Now, by plugging this data and the previous given data into the formula for the BMEP we get...

$$BMEP = \frac{Bhp \times 12 \text{ in/ft} \times 33000 \text{ ft-lbf/min} \times Z}{Cyl \text{ Area} \times Stroke \times n \times RPM}$$

$$BMEP = \frac{400 \times 12 \text{ in/ft} \times 33000 \text{ ft-lbf/min} \times 2}{13.3641 \text{ in}^2 \times 3.50 \text{ in} \times 8 \times 7000 \text{ rev/min}}$$

$$BMEP = \frac{4800 \text{ in/ft} \times 33000 \text{ ft-lbf/min} \times 2}{46.7744 \text{ in}^3 \times 8 \times 7000 \text{ rev/min}}$$

$$BMEP = \frac{158400000 \text{ in-lbf/min} \times 2}{374.1952 \text{ in}^3 \times 7000 \text{ rev/min}}$$

$$BMEP = \frac{316800000 \text{ in-lbf/min}}{2619366.400 \text{ in}^3\text{/min}}$$

$$BMEP = 120.9453 \text{ lbf/in}^2$$

THE MEAN EFFECTIVE pressure is not constant, but varies with changes in the rotational velocity(rpm) of the crankshaft. With increasing speed, the mean effective pressure achieves a maximum value and then tapers off to some extent sometime there afterwards.

CALCULATIONS

CHAPTER 14

BRAKE TORQUE

OTHER THAN horsepower, torque is the most frequently talked about element of engine performance. It is defined as a force applied on a rigid body at a perpendicular distance from a given point, and that has a tendency to cause a rotation about the same point(in this instance the center of the crankshaft). Stated otherwise, torque or moment of a force imparts to a rigid body a rotational motion about an axis perpendicular to the applied force (For instance: a crankshaft whereby the crank arm has a force applied to it

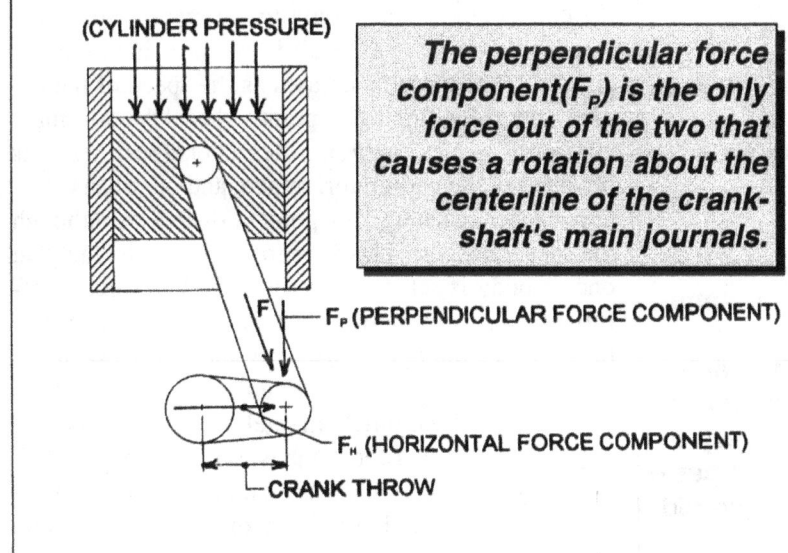

Figure 14-1: The pressure in the cylinder causes force to be exerted on top of the piston(s). This force(F) is transmitted to the connecting rod -- via the piston pin -- then to the crank arm. This force applied to the crank arm(crank throw) has two force components(F_H & F_P) during the power phase, except at top dead center(TDC) and bottom dead center(BDC). The horizontal force(F_H) shown below is also known as the parallel force component, because it always acts along the crank arm(passing through both centers of the crank's main and rod journals).

by the connecting rod as a result of the pressure exerted on top of each piston during the power stroke), as shown below.

THE CONNECTING ROD'S angle will change as a result of the rotational motion of the crankshaft. The effective turning force that causes the crankshaft to rotate is the perpendicular component of the applied force. It is measured from the centerline of the crankshaft, and is applied at the crankshaft's connecting rod journals.

THE FUNDAMENTAL EQUATIONS OF work and torque or moment of a force are ...

EQUATIONS(14a & 14b)

(14a) Work = Distance x Force

(14b) Torque = Force(F_p) x Distance

EXAMPLE(14a):
A simple illustration would be to assume that a stalled vehicle needed to be pushed in order to get it started. If a force of 100 lbf is necessary to cause the vehicle to move(and is also held constant), and if it was pushed through a distance of 50 feet, what was the amount of work done to get the vehicle started?

Work = Distance x Force
Work = 50 ft x 100 lbf
Work = 5000 ft-lbf

EXAMPLE(14b):
Another simple example; let's assume that you were trying to rotate your engine manually -- to adjust the valves -- by inserting a long handled 1.5 foot wrench on the center bolt that holds the crankshaft damper in place. If a force of 30 lbf were necessary to rotate the engine -- and were applied perpendicular to the wrench -- how much torque did it take to rotate the engine?

Torque = Force(F_p) x Distance
Torque = 30 lbf x 1.5
Torque = 45 lbf-ft

NOTE: Both equations 14a & 14b have the same units but the orders are reversed. The reasons being is that for work(equation 14a), the force is exerted *through* *a* *distance*, while for the torque(equation 14b), the force is applied *at* *a* *distance*.

ENGINE TORQUE IS the twisting or turning moment visualized as the work per unit of crankshaft rotation(measured in radians).

SINCE THERE ARE 2π **radians**($2 \times \pi = 2 \times 3.14159$ **radians** $= 6.28318$ **rad**) in **one entire revolution of 360 degrees**, then it follows that one radian(rad) is equal to 57.32^0. Engine torque is also the measure of an engine's ability to do work. For example, the ability to move a vehicle with a specified weight through some distance or to either push or pull a load over a desired distance.

SINCE TORQUE IS DEVELOPED by the forces exerted on top of the pistons and transmitted through the connecting rod assembly to the crankshaft, a net increase in torque will result if the force is further increased. The torque increases as the speed of the engine increases, up to a point where the air mass efficiency is maximum or when choke(peak) flow is obtained in the carburetor, intake, and/or exhaust system. After reaching that point it decreases although the speed persists. This is primary due to the fact that once a body is set in motion it takes less force or effort to keep it in motion than its initial resistance to being set in motion. *This resistance to being set in motion is called inertia.* Even though there exists some lack of essential air-fuel flow, there is still enough air and fuel for combustion to generate a sufficient amount of cylinder pressure. This pressure results in sufficient down force on top of the piston which keeps the engine speed on the increase.

ALSO, KEEP IN MIND THAT *A SMALL* body such as **a piston** can have a great momentum(the product of a mass, not weight, of a body times its velocity) if it travels at a high speed. A heavy body such as **a car** can have a large momentum even if it moves at a slow speed.

NOTE, THE BRAKE TORQUE IS EQUAL TO the indicated torque minus the frictional torque that is necessary to overcome friction, and other losses due to compression, etc.

THE TORQUE AND MEAN Effective pressure exhibit their peak values at the same engine speed. (If the torque vs rpm curve is relatively flat in relation to the torque's peak value, then there may not be a need for frequent gear changes.)

ONCE THE BRAKE MEAN EFFECTIVE pressure is known the brake torque can be found from the following equation...

$$\text{Brake Torque} = \frac{\text{Bmep} \times \text{Engine Displacement}}{Z \times 6.2832 \text{ rad} \times 12 \text{ in/ft}}$$

Bmep - Brake Mean Effective Pressure(lbf/in^2)

Z -- the number of revolutions necessary to to accomplish one power stroke per piston
- (Z = 1, for a two stroke engine)
- (Z = 2, for a four stroke engine)

Engine Displacement -- in cubic inches(in^3)

EXAMPLE(14c):
For an engine displacement of 360 cubic inches, and from EXAMPLE(13a) where:
Bmep = 125 lbf/in^2
Z = 2 rev(revolutions)
The brake torque output is therefore...

$$\text{Brake Torque} = \frac{\text{Bmep} \times \text{Engine Displacement}}{Z \times 6.2832 \text{ rad} \times 12 \text{ in/ft}}$$

$$\text{Brake Torque} = \frac{125 \text{ lbf/in}^2 \times 360 \text{ in}^3}{2 \text{ rev} \times 6.2832 \text{ rad} \times 12 \text{ in/ft}}$$

$$\text{Brake Torque} = \frac{45000 \text{ lbf-in}}{12.5664 \text{ rev} \times 12 \text{ in/ft}}$$

$$\text{Brake Torque} = \frac{45000 \text{ lbf-in}}{150.797 \text{ in/ft}}$$

Brake Torque = 298.414 lbf-ft

NOTE: Since the brake torque is calculated instead of the indicated torque, the brake mean effective pressure had to be used in the equation instead of the indicated mean effective pressure.

If the "Brake Torque" is calculated for a two(2) stroke engine where Z=1, the previous equation reduces to...

$$\text{Brake Torque} = \frac{\text{Bmep} \times \text{Engine Displacement}}{75.398 \text{ in/ft}}$$

If the "Brake Torque" is calculated for a four(4) stroke engine where Z=2, the previous equation reduces to...

$$\text{Brake Torque} = \frac{\text{Bmep} \times \text{Engine Displacement}}{150.797 \text{ in/ft}}$$

CHAPTER FOURTEEN

CALCULATIONS

CHAPTER 15

POWER! HORSEPOWER! BRAKE HORSEPOWER!

POWER

THE SEARCH FOR power is a seemingly never ending exploration. The more power an engine has, the more effective it is. This means that it possesses a greater potential to accomplish different or specific task(s). Before power can be attained the work and/or speed at which the work is done must be increased. Work is being done when an object is moving from one location to another location through lifting, pushing, or pulling on it.

Figure 15-1: Photo -- Courtesy of Pontiac Racing.

POWER IS THE rate at which work is done. The faster an object is moved(Figure 15-1), the more power it will have taken to move it, which says that power is the primary factor that determines how fast a vehicle can move. Power is calculated by dividing the work performed by the time it takes to perform the work, see the following equations.

Since,

Work = Force x Distance
Work -- is a force applied through a distance

- and -

Torque = Force(F_P) x Distance
Torque -- is a force applied at a distance

Then,

$$\text{Power} = \frac{\text{Work}}{\text{Time}} \quad \text{- or -} \quad \text{Power} = \frac{\text{Torque}}{\text{Time}}$$

- and -

$$\boxed{\text{Power} = \frac{\text{Force} \times \text{Distance}}{\text{Time}}}$$

EXAMPLE(15-1):
If a car were pushed by hand with a force of 200 lbf, over a distance of 50 feet, in 15 seconds, the amount of power necessary to accomplish this task would be...

$$\boxed{\text{Power} = \frac{\text{Distance} \times \text{Force}}{\text{Time}}}$$

$$\text{Power} = \frac{50 \text{ ft} \times 200 \text{ lbf}}{15 \text{ sec}}$$

$$\text{Power} = \frac{10000 \text{ ft-lbf}}{15 \text{ sec}}$$

Power = 666.67 ft-lbf/sec

- or -

15 seconds = 15 sec /(60 sec/minute)
15 seconds = .25 min

So,

$$\text{Power} = \frac{10000 \text{ ft-lbf}}{.25 \text{ min}}$$

Power = 40000 ft-lbf/min

HORSEPOWER

THE WORD *HORSEPOWER(HP)* OR one horsepower is equal to raising a weight of 550 lbs, a distance of 1 foot in a time of one second. Hence, one horsepower(1 hp) is equal to 550 foot-pound per second(550 ft-lbf/sec), which is equal to 33,000 foot-pounds per minute(33,000 ft-lbf/min). It can be stated that one horsepower is also equal to moving a 33,000 lb weight over a distance of one foot in a time of one minute, and second, a 1 lb weight transferred] throughout a distance of 33,000 feet in one minute(This concept can be applied to the 550 lb weight).

A UNIT OF ONE HORSEPOWER(HP) IS A standard quantity used for measuring and comparing horsepower. To find the horsepower of an engine, we therefore divide the work output per second or minute by 550 ft-lbf per second or 33,000 ft-lbf per min, as shown below.

HP = [Power(in seconds) / (550 ft-lbf/sec)]
HP = [Work/time(sec) / (550 ft-lbf/sec)]

- and -

HP = [Power(in minutes) / (33,000 ft-lbf/min)]
HP = [Work/time(min) / (33,000 ft-lbf/min)]

EXAMPLE(15-2):
Using the results from EXAMPLE(15a), the horsepower is...

$$\boxed{\text{Horsepower} = \frac{\text{Power(ft-lbf/sec)}}{550 \text{ ft-lbf/sec}}}$$

$$\text{Horsepower} = \frac{666.67 \text{ ft-lbf/sec}}{550 \text{ ft-lbf/sec}}$$

Horsepower = 1.21

- or -

$$\boxed{\text{Horsepower} = \frac{\text{Power(ft-lbf/min)}}{33000 \text{ ft-lbf/min}}}$$

$$\text{Horsepower} = \frac{40000 \text{ ft-lbf/min}}{33000 \text{ ft-lbf/min}}$$

Horsepower = 1.21

IT SHOULD BE NOTED THAT horsepower is a dimensionless number, because of the division that results in cancellation of units(ft-lbf/sec **--or--** ft-lbf/min)between the numerator and its denominator. It should be noted that horsepower is a function of the engine's cubic inch displacement, and speed.

BRAKE HORSEPOWER

INDICATED HORSEPOWER IS THE total horsepower developed in the engine, neglecting any power losses due to friction, etc. In reality, a part of the indicated horsepower developed by the burned air-fuel mixture is spent in overcoming mechanical and fluid friction due to bearings, pistons, mechanical fuel pumps, other mechanical parts of the engine, lubrication, the compression stroke, intake stroke, and exhaust stroke. The indicated horsepower minus these individual losses is called the *brake horsepower(BHP)*. Brake horsepower is of most importance and interest to the engine enthusiast, because this is the true power output that can be measured at the end of the crankshaft or flywheel.

THE EQUATION FOR THE brake horsepower is...

$$BHP = \frac{Bmep \times Stroke \times Cyl\ Area \times n \times N}{33000\ ft\text{-}lbf/min \times 12\ in/ft \times Z}$$

BHP = brake horsepower(has no units)
Bmep = brake mean effective pressure(lb/in^2)
Stroke -- given in inches(in)
Cyl Area = cylinder area(in^2)
n = the number of cylinders
N = engine speed, rev/min(rpm)
Z = number of revolutions necessary to complete one cycle of engine operation or one power stroke(Z = 2, for a four stroke engine)

EXAMPLE(15-3):
An 8-cylinder four stroke engine with a brake mean effective pressure(Bmep) of 160 lbf/in^2 at 5600 rpm, a 4.125" bore, and 3.75" stroke, will have a brake horsepower equal to...

Cyl Area = 0.7854 x Bore x Bore
Cyl Area = 0.7854 x 4.125 in x 4.125 in
Cyl Area = 0.7854 x 17.0156 in^2
Cyl Area = 13.3641 in^2

(Stroke x Cyl Area) = 3.75 in x 13.3641 in^2
(Stroke x Cyl Area) = 50.1154 in^3

$$BHP = \frac{Bmep \times (Stroke \times Cyl\ Area) \times n \times N}{33000\ ft\text{-}lbf/min \times 12\ in/ft \times Z}$$

$$BHP = \frac{160\ lbf/in^2 \times 50.1154\ in^3 \times 8 \times 5600\ rpm}{33000\ ft\text{-}lbf/min \times 12\ in/ft \times 2}$$

$$BHP = \frac{8018.4640\ lbf\text{-}in \times 8 \times 5600\ rev/min}{396000\ lbf\text{-}in/min \times 2}$$

$$BHP = \frac{64147.7120\ lbf\text{-}in \times 5600\ rev/min}{792000\ lbf\text{-}in/min}$$

$$BHP = \frac{359227187.2\ \cancel{lbf\text{-}in/min}}{792000\ \cancel{lbf\text{-}in/min}}$$

BHP = 453.5697

In order to calculate the brake horsepower(BHP) using the *horsepower equivalent* of **550 ft-lbf/sec**, the engine speed(N) in **rpm(rev/min)** must be converted to **rps(rev/sec)**. To do this, divide the **rpm** by **60 sec/min**(Example: rpm/(60 sec/min) = rps). As a result, the equation for the brake horsepower will resemble the following.

$$BHP = \frac{Bmep \times Stroke \times Cyl\ Area \times n \times (N/60)}{550\ ft\text{-}lbf/sec \times 12\ in/ft \times Z}$$

NOTE: Since the <u>brake</u> horsepower is calculated instead of the <u>indicated</u> horsepower, the <u>brake</u> mean effective pressure had to be used in the equation instead of the <u>indicated</u> mean effective pressure.

CALCULATIONS

CHAPTER 16

CAMSHAFTS

(Principles, Valve Timing & Valve Events)

THIS CHAPTER WILL BE strictly limited to the spark ignition, four stroke, normally aspirated, internal combustion engine.

WHETHER YOU ARE BUILDING, rebuilding, overhauling, or modifying an engine, the one component that is a major focal point of engine performance is the camshaft. What we call a cam and lifter is explained in kinematics of engineering as a *cam* and *follower*.

SELECTING A PROPER OR SUITABLE camshaft can raise some very interesting questions for the engine builder, such as:

(1) What should the maximum and minimum rpm limit be(rpm range)?

(2) How much duration, lift, lobe center angle, etc. is essential to optimizing the engine's performance over this desired rpm range?

(3) Finally, should the camshaft grind be hydraulic, solid lifter, etc.?

HOWEVER, THESE choices will depend highly upon the vehicles usage and other factors such as:

> **Just because the cubic inch displacements of two or more engines happen to be equivalent or almost equivalent, does not mean that the same camshaft will work properly in each application.**

vehicle weight, engine displacement, type of transmission, compression ratio, rear end gear ratio, intake and exhaust systems, and sometimes it may not require any more than simply replacing the existing camshaft with a new camshaft that is identical in specifications.

CAREFUL ATTENTION SHOULD BE TAKEN BEFORE copying someone else's camshaft selection. Just because the cubic inch displacements of two or more engines happen to be equivalent or almost equivalent, does not mean that the same camshaft will work properly in each application. The intrinsic characteristics may differ dramatically, meaning the parameters of an engine's internal parts(cylinders, cylinder head's intake ports & exhaust ports, intake manifold, carburetor(s), or fuel injection) may vary quite considerably. The cylinder heads e.g., some have large intake ports and small exhaust ports, while others have small intake ports and large exhaust ports.

Cylinder heads exhibiting large intake ports and small exhaust ports may require a camshaft with more duration on the exhaust side than on the intake side. This allows more time for the exhaust gases to escape. Heads exhibiting small intake ports and large exhaust ports may require a camshaft with more duration on the intake side than on the exhaust side. This increases the time necessary to fill the cylinders to offset the losses caused by fluid friction.

Cam Lobe Profile Terms & Definitions (Figure 16a)

- **BASE CIRCLE** -- This is where the lifter is located when the valve is completely closed, and is also the reference point from which the clearance ramps and other lobe features are measured.
- **HEEL** -- The part of the base circle that is opposite of nose, and is indicative of zero valve lift.
- **OPENING CLEARANCE RAMPS** -- These ramps serve to slowly or gently, as necessary, take up clearance or lash in the valvetrain, and initiates the acceleration of the lifter and other related valvetrain components.
- **CLOSING CLEARANCE RAMPS** -- These ramps on the opposite side of the cam lobe serve to slowly and gently, as necessary, lower the valve on its seat in order to prevent it from bouncing.
- **FLANKS** -- The portions of the cam lobe that rapidly accelerates the opening and closing of the valves, respectively.
- **NOSE** -- The point of the cam lobe where maximum valve lift occurs.
- **LOBE LIFT** -- The distance the lifter is raised above the base circle.

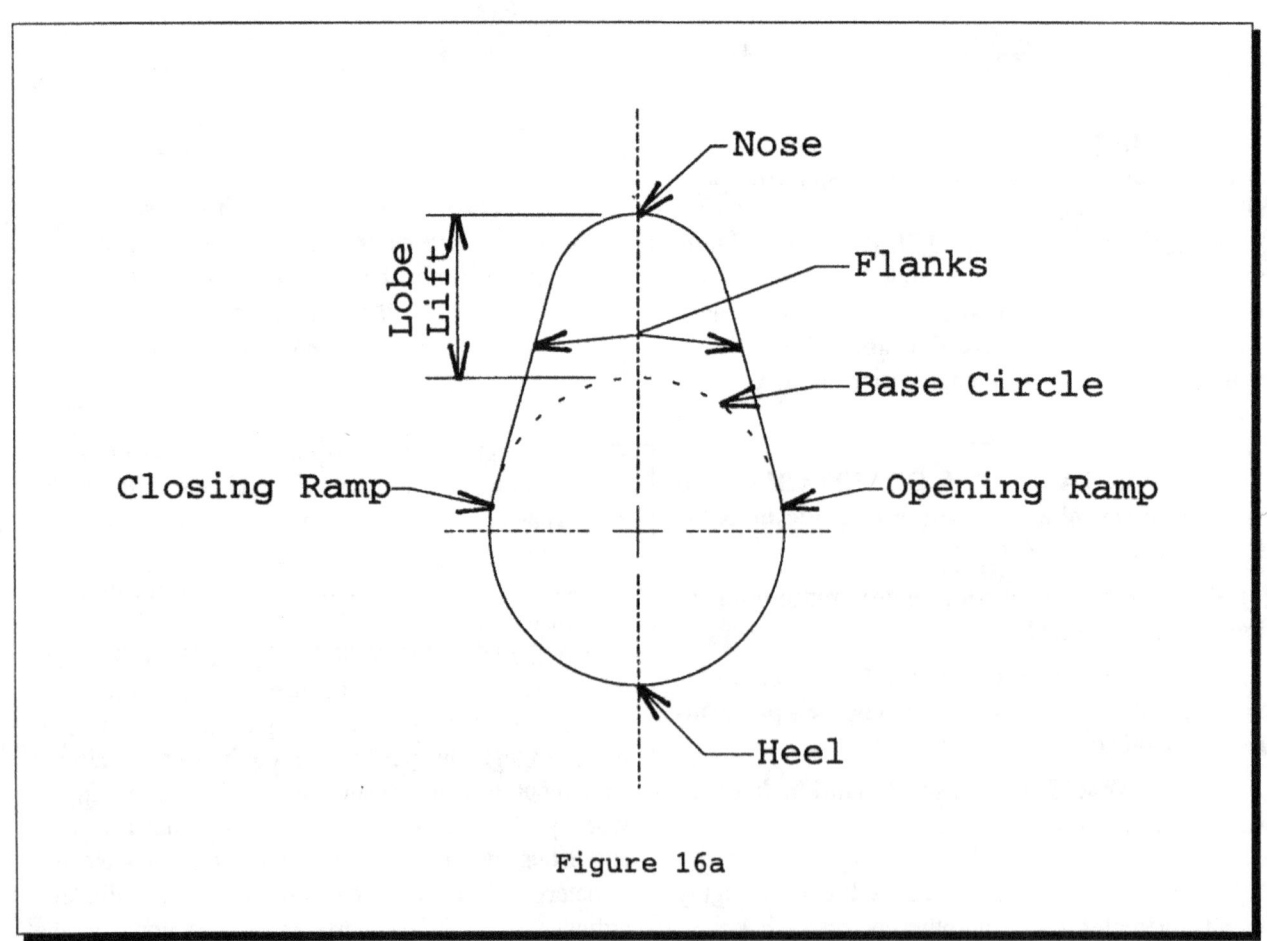

Figure 16a

Camshaft Lobe Specifications Terms & Definitions

- **DURATION** -- The amount of time in degrees of crankshaft rotation that the valve is off its seat(Figure 16c & 16d).

- **DURATION @.050" LOBE LIFT** -- The amount of time remaining in degrees of crankshaft rotation after the cam lobe has raised the lifter a distance of .050" above the base circle(Figure 16e).

- **INTAKE OPENING TIME** -- The number of degrees of crankshaft rotation that the intake valve opens before the piston reaches top dead center(BTDC), which occurs during the latter part of the exhaust stroke(Figure 16b, 16c, 16d, 16e, & 16f).

- **INTAKE CLOSING TIME** -- The number of degrees of crankshaft rotation by which the piston has moved away from bottom dead center(ABDC), which occurs in most cases during the early part of the compression stroke(Figure 16b, 16c, 16d, 16e, & 16f).

- **EXHAUST OPENING TIME** -- The number of degrees of crankshaft rotation that the exhaust valve begins to open before the piston has reached bottom dead center(BBDC), during the latter part power stroke(Figure 16b, 16c, 16d, 16e, & 16f).

- **EXHAUST CLOSING TIME** -- The number of degrees of crankshaft rotation by which the piston has moved away from top dead center(ATDC), during the initial part of the intake stroke(Figure 16b, 16c, 16d, 16e, & 16f).

- **OVERLAP** -- The total number of degrees of crankshaft rotation that the intake valve and exhaust valves are off their respective seats, simultaneously. This is the number of degrees of crankshaft rotation that the intake valve opens before top dead center(BTDC) plus the number of degrees the exhaust valve closes after top dead center(ATDC) (Figure 16d, 16e, & 16f).

- **LOBE LIFT** -- The amount of distance that the lifter is raised above the base circle(Figure 16b).

- **VALVE LIFT** -- Although this is not a lobe specification, but is related to it, it is defined as the amount of distance that the valve is raised off its seat(Figure 16e).

- **INTAKE LOBE CENTERLINE** -- This is the number of crankshaft degrees that the center of the intake lobe should lie ATDC when installed in the engine(Figure 16e & 16f).

- **EXHAUST LOBE CENTERLINE** -- This is the number of crankshaft degrees that the center of the exhaust lobe should lie BTDC when installed in the engine(Figure 16e & 16f).

- **LOBE SEPARATION ANGLE** -- This is the number of <u>camshaft</u> degrees between the centerlines of the intake and exhaust lobes for crankshaft degrees, and divided by <u>2</u> for camshaft degrees(Figure 16e & 16f).

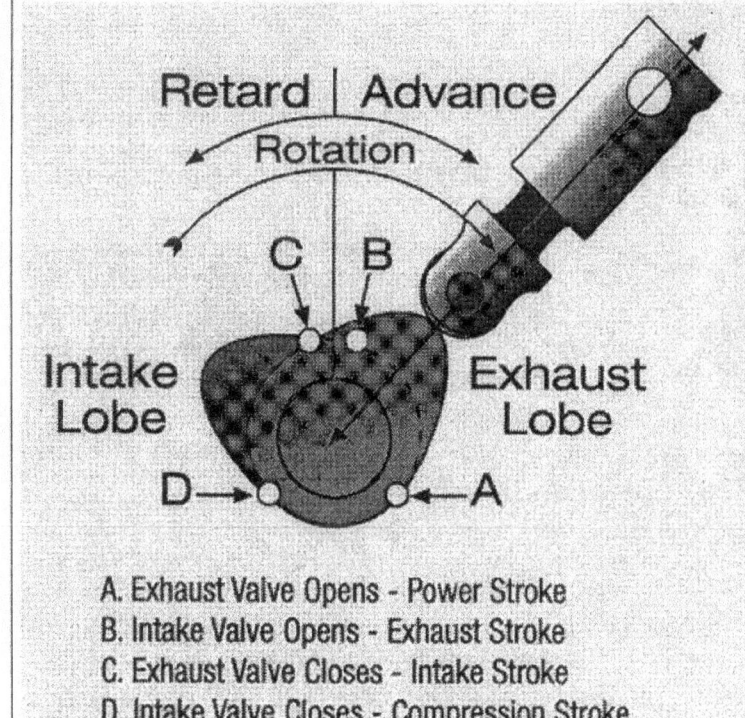

A. Exhaust Valve Opens - Power Stroke
B. Intake Valve Opens - Exhaust Stroke
C. Exhaust Valve Closes - Intake Stroke
D. Intake Valve Closes - Compression Stroke

Figure 16b:

This illustration to the left shows that:

1) at point <u>A</u>, the exhaust valve opens BBDC or near end of the power stroke;

2) at point <u>B</u>, the intake valve opens BTDC or near end of exhaust stroke;

3) at point <u>C</u>, the exhaust valve closes ATDC or during early part of the intake stroke;

4) at point <u>D</u>, the intake valve closes ABDC or during the early part of the compression stroke.

Illustration -- Courtesy of COMPCams

- Duration -

FIRST, THE TYPE OF valves associated with the current cam mechanisms are called *poppet valves*.

THE CLEARANCES WITHIN THE valvetrain(between camshaft, rocker arm, and valve) must be slowly taken up and the valve lifted slowly initially, if noise and wear are to be kept to a minimum. Also, the valve should not be closed rapidly, to avoid bouncing on its seat.

IT IS ALSO IMPORTANT TO NOTE That there exist two kinds of cam lobe patterns:

- **Single Pattern** -- This is when the lift and duration of the intake and exhaust lobes are the same.
- **Dual Pattern** -- This is when the lift and or duration on the intake and exhaust lobes are not the same.

NOW, DURATION HAS a profound impact on an engine's performance, in that its purpose is to hold the valve open long enough to allow sufficient time for the air-fuel mixture to charge the cylinders, and for the exhaust to expel itself. In addition, if the engine's rpm limit is increased, an extension of the duration is needed in order for proper charging and exhausting of the cylinders to take place. Something to note is that as the engine speed rises there is less time for the air-fuel mixture to enter and to exit the cylinder(s), therefore, the valves must be held open longer to complement this increase. Also, the required amount of duration is dependent upon the efficiency of the intake and exhaust systems. More restriction on either side or both sides can impede the flow entering and/or leaving the cylinder, thus, affecting the duration requirement(s). Duration is also affected by the pressure differences in the intake and exhaust systems, and the pressure in the cylinder during the power stroke. The *intake* and *exhaust durations* are computed by adding the opening and closing times to 180^0.

$$\text{Intake Duration} = IO + 180^0 + IC$$

I O -- Intake Opening Time
I C -- Intake Closing Time

$$\text{Exhaust Duration} = EO + 180^0 + EC$$

E O -- Exhaust Opening Time
E C -- Exhaust Closing Time

EXAMPLE(16-1a):
If a cam's intake lobe opening time is 45^0 BTDC, and the intake closing time is 77^0 ABDC, the intake duration will be...

$$\text{Intake Duration} = IO + 180^0 + IC$$

$$\text{Intake Duration} = 45^0 + 180^0 + 77^0$$

$$\text{Intake Duration} = 302^0$$

EXAMPLE(16-1b):
If a cam's exhaust lobe opening time is 84^0 BBDC, and the exhaust closing time is 52^0 ATDC, the exhaust duration will be...

$$\text{Exhaust Duration} = EO + 180^0 + EC$$

$$\text{Exhaust Duration} = 84^0 + 180^0 + 52^0$$

$$\text{Exhaust Duration} = 316^0$$

- Duration @ .050" Lobe Lift -

THIS IS THE DURATION AT which effective(adequate) flow will begin at the valve. If the number of degrees of crankshaft rotation are known at this lobe lift, a better analysis of the mass flow rate of <u>air-fuel mixture & exhaust</u> entering and exiting the cylinder, respectively, can be performed. This does take the efficiencies of both the intake and exhaust systems into account(see Figure 16e).

- Intake Opening Time(I O) -

AN ENGINE'S torque or work output is directly reliant upon the internal energy present minus any heat loss during the combustion process of the air-fuel mixture. Air fills most of the cylinder's volume in relation to the amount of fuel inducted. Therefore, it follows that any reduction in air flow due to fluid friction between the air and intake port will hamper

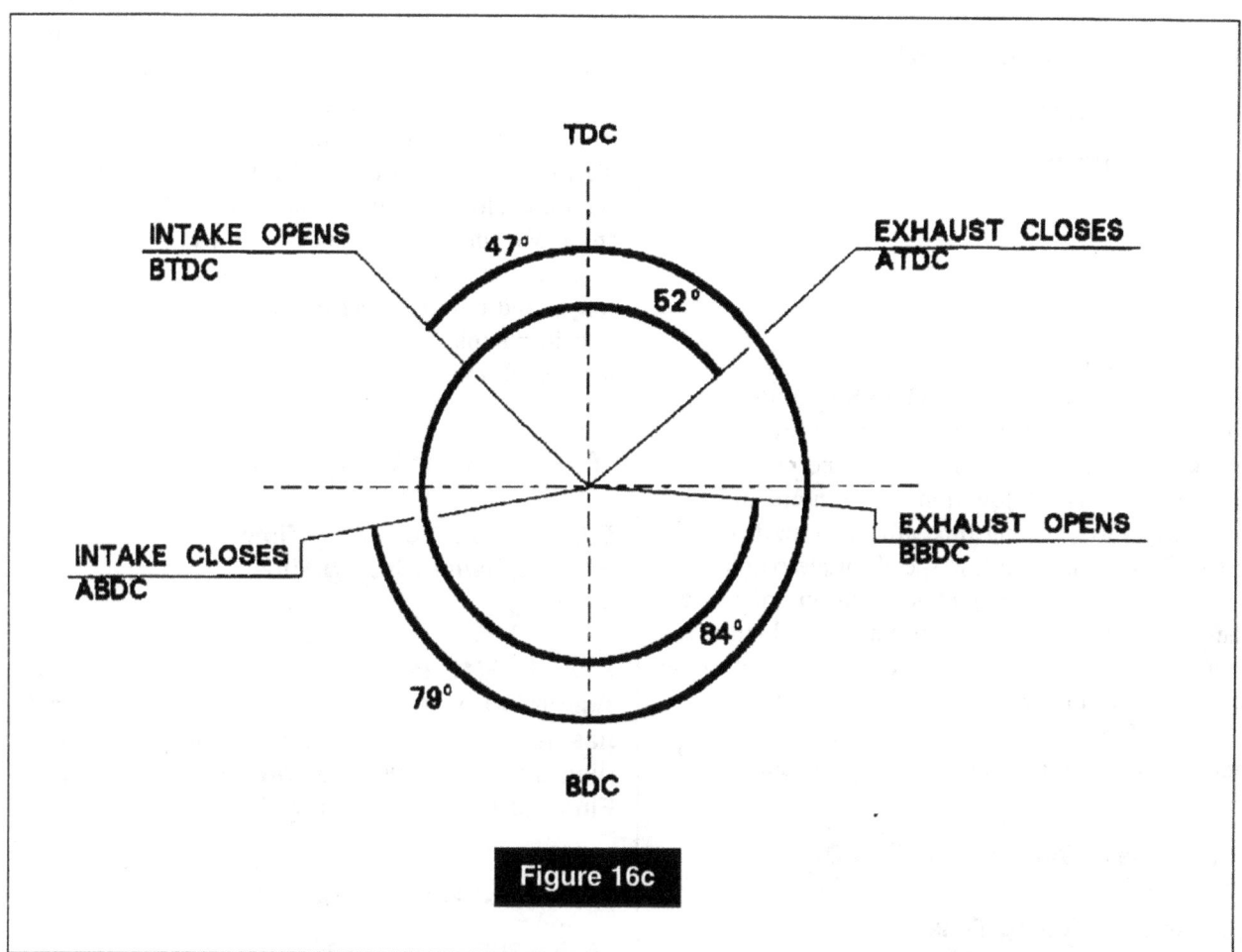

Figure 16c

the performance. So, if the engine's air consumption is reduced, adding an excessive amount of fuel will not result in any further increase in torque or power output. Therefore, the greater the unit air charge(the amount of air inducted per intake stroke per cylinder), the greater will be the potential to produce more torque.

IT IS widely accepted to start by opening the intake valve BTDC during the latter part of the exhaust stroke(Figure 16d, 16e, & 16f). The intake's flow area is smaller, allowing time for the air flow to get started. Also, when the piston speed is at its maximum, it is acceptable to have the valve fully opened. Nevertheless, it should be noted that while the intake valve is starting to open the exhaust valve is slowly closing before and/or after top dead center. This reduces a major rise in exhaust pressure that could result in back pressure and backflow of exhaust residuals into each of the intake ports. Since both of the valves are part open BTDC & ATDC(at the end of the exhaust stroke and beginning of the intake stroke), they are said to be *overlapped*. One might think that the intake valve and exhaust valve are again overlapped at bottom dead center when looking at the valve timing diagram, but they are not. Because, very close examination of the valve timing diagram should and will prove that this is not so. Also, there exist no acute, 90^0, or obtuse lobe separation angle that would generate any valve overlap period at both TDC and BDC, sequentially.

$$I\,O = \text{Intake Duration} - 180^0 - I\,C$$

I O -- Intake Opening Time
I C -- Intake Closing Time

EXAMPLE(16-2a):
If a camshaft with a 282^0 intake duration had an intake closing time of 68^0 ABDC, what would the intake opening time be?

CHAPTER SIXTEEN

$$IO = \text{Intake Duration} - 180° - IC$$

$$IO = 282° - 180° - 68°$$

$$IO = 34° \text{ BTDC}$$

- Intake Closing Time(I C) -

THE INTAKE VALVE STAYS open during the initial part of the compression stroke in order for extended charging of the cylinders to take place(Figure 16d, 16e, & 16f). A low rpm engine normally has a very early valve closing time after bottom dead center(ABDC) to enhance low speed torque output, and reduce the dynamic compression ratio in order to eschew auto-ignition that leads to knock. A high speed engine normally closes its intake valves sometime later than that of the low speed engines, to increase charging of the cylinder(s), which results from the increase in momentum of the incoming air-fuel mixture.

$$IC = \text{Intake Duration} - 180° - IO$$

I C -- Intake Closing Time
I O -- Intake Opening Time

EXAMPLE(16-2b):
If an engine builder wanted an intake opening time of 44° BTDC, but wanted to keep the intake duration at 300°, the intake closing time would have to be...

$$IC = \text{Intake Duration} - 180° - IO$$

$$IC = 300° - 180° - 44°$$

$$IC = 76° \text{ ABDC}$$

-Exhaust Opening Time(E O) -

BEFORE THE POWER stroke is terminated, the exhaust valve starts to open before bottom dead center. This permits exhaust blowdown to take place, which allows the gases to escape primarily on their own as a result of the pressure in the cylinder. Part of the available energy is lost during the power stroke as a result of the early opening of the exhaust valve. This is a waste at low speeds(idle, off-idle, and part throttle). However, as the engine's speed is increased from part throttle(low speed) to wide open throttle(high and or full speed), there is a net gain in the torque and power output that results from the reduction in pumping effort by the piston during the exhaust stroke(Figure 16d, 16e, & 16f).

$$EO = \text{Exhaust Duration} - 180° - EC$$

E O -- Exhaust Opening Time
E C -- Exhaust Closing Time

EXAMPLE(16-3a):
Assuming a camshaft with a 6000 rpm limit has an exhaust duration of 300°, accompanied by an exhaust closing time of 56° ATDC. Find the exhaust opening time.

$$EO = \text{Exhaust Duration} - 180° - EC$$

$$EO = 300° - 180° - 56°$$

$$EO = 64° \text{ BBDC}$$

- Exhaust Closing Time(E C) -

IF THE exhaust valve(s) were closed slightly before top dead center, or at TDC at the end of the exhaust stroke, scavenging of the exhaust gases would be greatly hindered. An increase in reversion of the intake charge would be evident due to a partial pressure build up resulting from the compression of the exhaust gas remnants in the combustion chamber. Nonetheless, it has been characteristic of performance engine building to close the exhaust valve after the piston has moved away from top dead center during the initial phase of the intake stroke to reduce these effects that take place at low and high engine velocities(Figure 16d, 16e, & 16f).

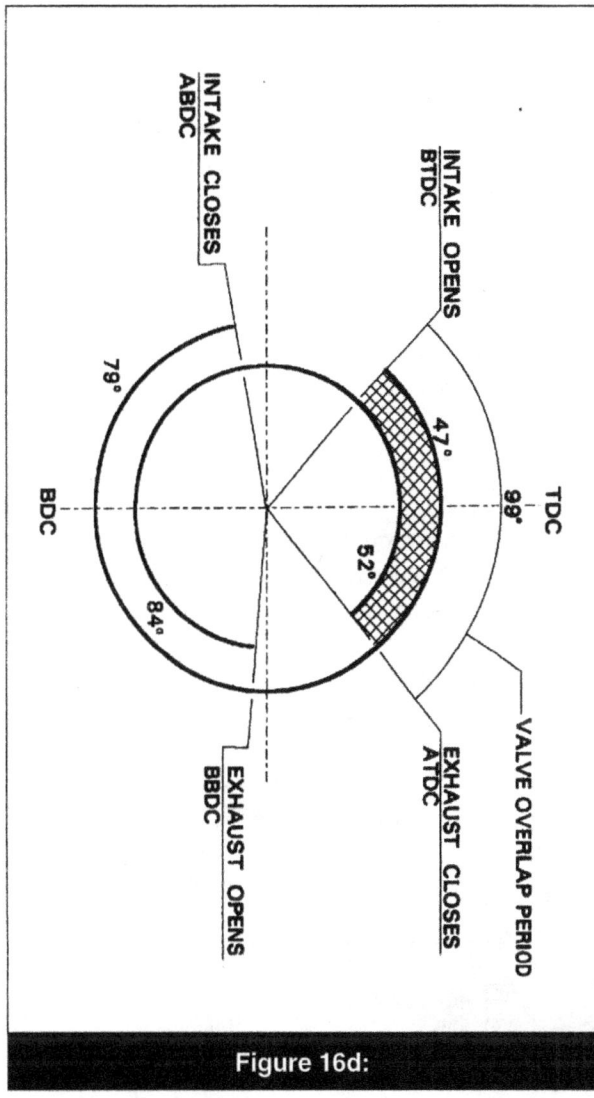

Figure 16d:

$$EC = \text{Exhaust Duration} - 180° - EO$$

E C -- Exhaust Closing Time
E O -- Exhaust Opening Time

EXAMPLE(16-3b):
Assuming a 7000 rpm engine has an exhaust duration of 290°, accompanied by an exhaust opening time of 70° BBDC. Find the exhaust closing time.

$$EC = \text{Exhaust Duration} - 180° - EO$$

$$EC = 290° - 180° - 70°$$

$$EC = 40° \text{ ATDC}$$

- Valve Overlap Period(Figure 16d, 16e, & 16f) -

AS THE PEAK design engine speed is raised or lowered it becomes necessary to increase or decrease the amount of valve overlap, respectively. The reason being is that as the desirable peak engine rpm (speed) is raised it becomes extremely vital to increase the overlap to optimize the engine's torque and power output. This is done by opening the intake valves earlier BTDC near the end of the compression stroke and closing the exhaust valve later ATDC during the intake stroke. If the exhaust system has been relieved of all of its major restrictions such as the converters/mufflers and too small of a pipe diameter, the overlap can be increased because there is less restriction to the exhaust flow, and stated otherwise, there is less back pressure.

$$\text{Valve Overlap Period} = IO + EC$$

I O -- Intake Opening Time
E C -- Exhaust Closing Time

EXAMPLE(16-4):
Consider a camshaft with the following lobe specifications: intake opens 30° BTDC, intake closes 62° ABDC, exhaust opens 70° BBDC, and exhaust closes 28° ATDC. Compute the overlap from the given data.

Since the overlap is a function of the intake opening time, and exhaust closing time, it follows that:

$$\text{Valve Overlap Period} = IO + EC$$

$$\text{Valve Overlap Period} = 30° + 28°$$

$$\text{Valve Overlap Period} = 58°$$

- Lobe Lift & Valve Lift -

LOBE LIFT IS SIMPLY The distance a tappet or lifter is raised above the cam's base circle or, the distance measured from the base circle to the nose of the cam lobe. The amount of lobe lift is usually determined by the cam designer. On the other hand, valve lift is a valve event that is a function of the lobe lift and rocker arm ratio; meaning that the product of the lobe lift and the rocker arm ratio dictates the overall valve lift. The rate of valve lift(which is not a lobe specification) is determined by the cam lobe profile and rocker arm ratio. So, for any lobe lift and lobe profile design--when comparing two or more camshaft lobes--the lobe specifications are held constant, the valve lift and rate of valve lift are then a major function of the rocker arm ratio! Valve lift provides an opening between the valve and its seat to allow passage of the air-fuel mixture into the cylinder, and exhaust products out of the cylinder. In addition, the time it takes to fill the cylinder is affected also by the valve's diameter, the engine's speed, and also, the pressure difference across the valve. It follows that the rate by which the valve is raised off its seat determines how quickly the air-fuel mixture can enter the cylinder. In other words, the faster the valve opens, the sooner the cylinder will be charged with a greater amount of mixture. Also, the larger the rocker arm ratio, the faster the valve will be raised above its seat. So, the valve lift equation is as follows:

Valve Lift = Lobe lift x Rocker Arm Ratio

Example(16-5a):
A 280^0 duration cam has a lobe lift of .345 inches. What would the valve lift be if first a 1.6:1 rocker arm ratio were used in the engine, and then later on a 1.65:1 ratio were substituted into the engine?

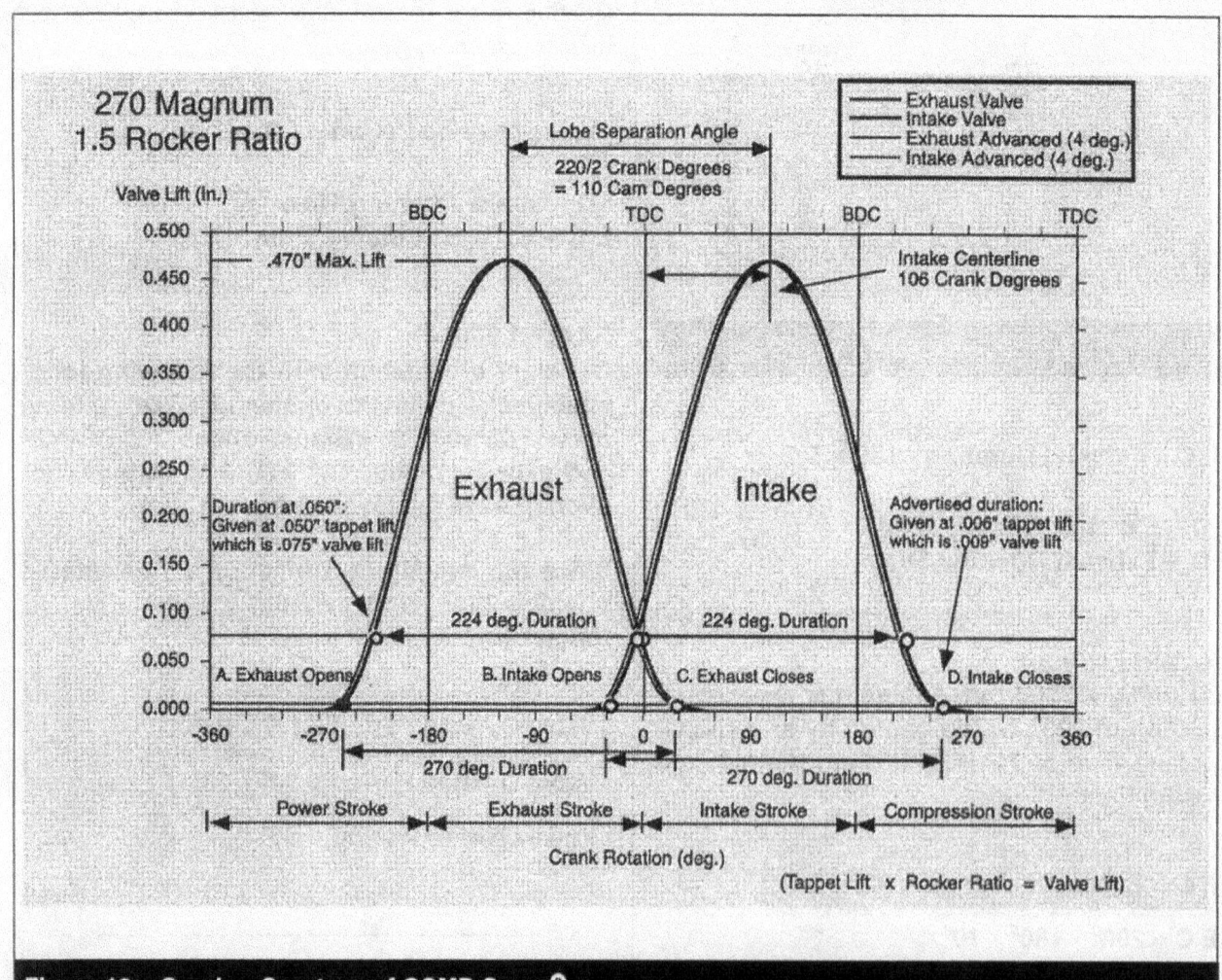

Figure 16e: Graph -- Courtesy of COMP Cams®

(1) For the 1.6 rocker arm ratio:

$$\text{Valve Lift} = \text{Lobe Lift} \times \text{Rocker Arm Ratio}$$

Valve Lift = .345 in x 1.6

Valve Lift = .552 in

(2) For the 1.65 rocker arm ratio:

$$\text{Valve Lift} = \text{Lobe Lift} \times \text{Rocker Arm Ratio}$$

Valve Lift = .345 in x 1.65

Valve Lift = .569 in

IF YOU DESIRE TO KNOW the *lobe lift* for a practical *rocker arm ratio* and *valve lift*, you can use the following equation.

$$\text{Lobe lift} = \frac{\text{Valve Lift}}{\text{Rocker Arm Ratio}}$$

Example(16-5b):
If an engine combination were to have a practical valve lift of .575 inches, and you desire to use a 1.70 rocker arm ratio, the lobe lift for these conditions would be...

$$\text{Lobe lift} = \frac{\text{Valve Lift}}{\text{Rocker Arm Ratio}}$$

$$\text{Lobe lift} = \frac{.575 \text{ in}}{1.70}$$

Lobe lift = .338 in

- **Intake Lobe Centerline** -

BESIDES BEING THE GUIDE for installing the camshaft in the engine, the intake lobe centerline is the angle at which the maximum valve lift occurs(The angle at which maximum valve lift applies to the following section on the exhaust lobe centerline also.). It is very important when considering the piston's maximum velocity relative to this angle--that is measured after top dead center(ATDC) -- see Figures 16e & 16f. Note, this could recommend that the camshaft be installed at some other angle, other than that of the calculated lobe centerline! See the equation that is shown below.

$$\text{Intake Centerline} = \frac{IC - IO + 180°}{2}$$

I C -- Intake Closing Time
I O -- Intake Opening Time

EXAMPLE(16-6a):
If an intake lobe's opening and closing times are 34° BTDC and 70° ABDC, respectively. Find the centerline of the intake cam's lobe.

$$\text{Intake Centerline} = \frac{IC - IO + 180°}{2}$$

$$\text{Intake Centerline} = \frac{70° - 34° + 180°}{2}$$

$$\text{Intake Centerline} = \frac{36° + 180°}{2}$$

$$\text{Intake Centerline} = \frac{216°}{2}$$

Intake Centerline = 108° ATDC

- **Exhaust Lobe Centerline** -

THE EXHAUST CENTERLINE(see Figure 16e & 16f) IS generally taken into consideration when the camshaft is advanced or retarded(no split overlap -- where the intake opening and closing times are not equal). If the exhaust centerline is greater than the intake's centerline, the camshaft will be advanced. This will advance the exhaust valve timing events in relation to top dead center. If the exhaust centerline is less than the intake's centerline, the camshaft is retarded. This will delay the exhaust valve timing events in relation to top dead center. The previous statements regarding advancing and retarding the camshaft apply to the intake lobe's centerline as well. See the following equation.

$$\text{Exhaust Centerline} = \frac{EO - EC + 180°}{2}$$

E O -- Exhaust Opening Time
E C -- Exhaust Closing Time

EXAMPLE(16-6b):
Consider the following exhaust valve timing events, and find the centerline of the exhaust cam's lobe.

Given: The exhaust valve opens at $80°$ BBDC and closes $40°$ ATDC.

$$\text{Exhaust Centerline} = \frac{EO - EC + 180°}{2}$$

$$\text{Exhaust Centerline} = \frac{80° - 40° + 180°}{2}$$

$$\text{Exhaust Centerline} = \frac{40° + 180°}{2}$$

$$\text{Exhaust Centerline} = \frac{40° + 180°}{2}$$

$$\text{Exhaust Centerline} = \frac{220°}{2}$$

$$\text{Exhaust Centerline} = 110° \text{ BTDC}$$

- Lobe Separation Angle -

THE LOBE SEPARATION ANGLE IS the number of degrees between the point of maximum lift(lobe centerline) on the intake lobe and the point of maximum lift(lobe centerline) on the exhaust lobe for any given cylinder(Figure 16e). *This angle is the only angle measured in camshaft degrees.* All other cam lobe specifications are given in crankshaft degrees.

A CAMSHAFT HAVING A CLOSER LOBE SEPARATION angle(s) will theoretically, produce more mid-range to top end power than the same cam with a wider lobe separation angle. Since a constricted lobe separation angle increases the valve overlap period, the incoming air-fuel charge will assist in expelling the remaining portions of exhaust residuals from the cylinder and combustion chamber. Narrow lobe separation angles result in the valves being opened and closed while the piston is closer to top dead center, so it is good to be careful about the valve--to--piston clearance.

WIDE LOBE SEPARATION angles will yield or produce better low to mid-range rpm torque and less top end power than the same cam with a narrower lobe separation angle. Since an increased lobe separation angle decreases the valve overlap period.

IF A CAMSHAFT IS GROUND neither advanced nor retarded, both intake and exhaust centerlines will be equal, and, each one's valve timing centerlines will be identical to the lobe separation angle. However, if a camshaft is ground advanced -- resulting in the closing of the intake valves earlier, which builds cylinder pressure more quickly, and therefore, gives a better low end torque -- the intake centerline will be less than the exhaust centerline. If the camshaft is ground retarded -- resulting in the opening of the exhaust valve later, which increases the negative pumping work of the piston during the exhaust stroke -- the exhaust centerline will be than the intake centerline.

SELECTING THE RIGHT camshaft will depend also on the mixture velocity, rod angularity, bore-to-stroke ratio, and the engine's static compression ratio.

THE LOBE SEPARATION ANGLE IS equal to the intake's lobe centerline plus the exhaust lobe centerline divided by two as shown below.

$$\text{Lobe Sep Angle} = \frac{\text{Intake CL} + \text{Exhaust CL}}{2}$$

Lobe Sep Angle -- Lobe Separation Angle
Intake CL -- Intake Centerline
Exhaust CL -- Exhaust Centerline

EXAMPLE(16-7):
An intake lobe centerline of $108°$, and an exhaust lobe centerline of $112°$, will yield a camshaft's lobe separation angle of...

$$\text{Lobe Sep Angle} = \frac{\text{Intake CL} + \text{Exhaust CL}}{2}$$

$$\text{Lobe Sep Angle} = \frac{108° + 112°}{2}$$

$$\text{Lobe Sep Angle} = \frac{220°}{2}$$

$$\text{Lobe Sep Angle} = 110°$$

EXAMPLE(16-8):
If the lobe separation angle is $112°$, and the exhaust lobe centerline is $110°$, calculate the intake lobe centerline.

$$\text{Intake C L} = (2 \times \text{Lobe Sep Angle}) - \text{Exh CL}$$

$$\text{Intake C L} = (2 \times 112°) - 110°$$

$$\text{Intake C L} = 224° - 110°$$

$$\text{Intake C L} = 114°$$

Intake CL -- Intake Centerline
Lobe Sep Angle -- Lobe Separation Angle
Exhaust CL -- Exhaust Centerline

EXAMPLE(16-9):
If the lobe separation angle is $108°$, and the intake lobe centerline is $106°$, calculate the exhaust lobe centerline.

$$\text{Exh C L} = (2 \times \text{Lobe Sep Angle}) - \text{Intake CL}$$

$$\text{Exh C L} = (2 \times 108°) - 106°$$

$$\text{Exh C L} = 216° - 106°$$

$$\text{Exh C L} = 110°$$

Intake CL -- Intake Centerline
Lobe Sep Angle -- Lobe Separation Angle
Exhaust CL(Exh CL) -- Exhaust Centerline

- Cylinder Under Pressure -

IT MAY BE THOUGHT THAT THE longer the cylinder remains pressurized during the power stroke--while combustion of the air-fuel mixture is taking place -- the greater will be the magnitude of the torque and power output. On the contrary, the longer the cylinder is under pressure, a reduction in time-- that is essential for scavenging of the engine's combustion chamber--will exist during the entire exhaust phase. The pumping work will also be increased to help rid the cylinder and combustion chamber of the residual exhaust gases left behind.

FURTHER OBSERVATION OF PROLONGING THE power phase will show that as the piston descends, there will also be a corresponding decrease in pressure and temperature resulting from the expansion of the burned and/or burning air-fuel mixture. Due to this phenomenon, it becomes quite essential to open the exhaust valve earlier during the power stroke to take advantage of the higher cylinder pressure that enhances scavenging of the cylinder and combustion chamber. This subsequently results in an increase in exhaust velocity.

ONCE THE CRANKSHAFT HAS rotated through an angle of $90°$ or slightly greater, the amount of force exerted on the crank arm begins to significantly decrease, resulting in a degradation in the torque's output for that cylinder.

THE INCREASED SCAVENGING OF THE exhaust gases will help to draw the intake charge -- air-fuel mixture -- into the cylinder preceding and during the initial phase of the intake stroke.

CYLINDER UNDER PRESSURE IS DEFINED AS *the time from which the intake valve closes during the compression stroke, to the time when the exhaust valve opens during the power stroke(Figure 16f)*.

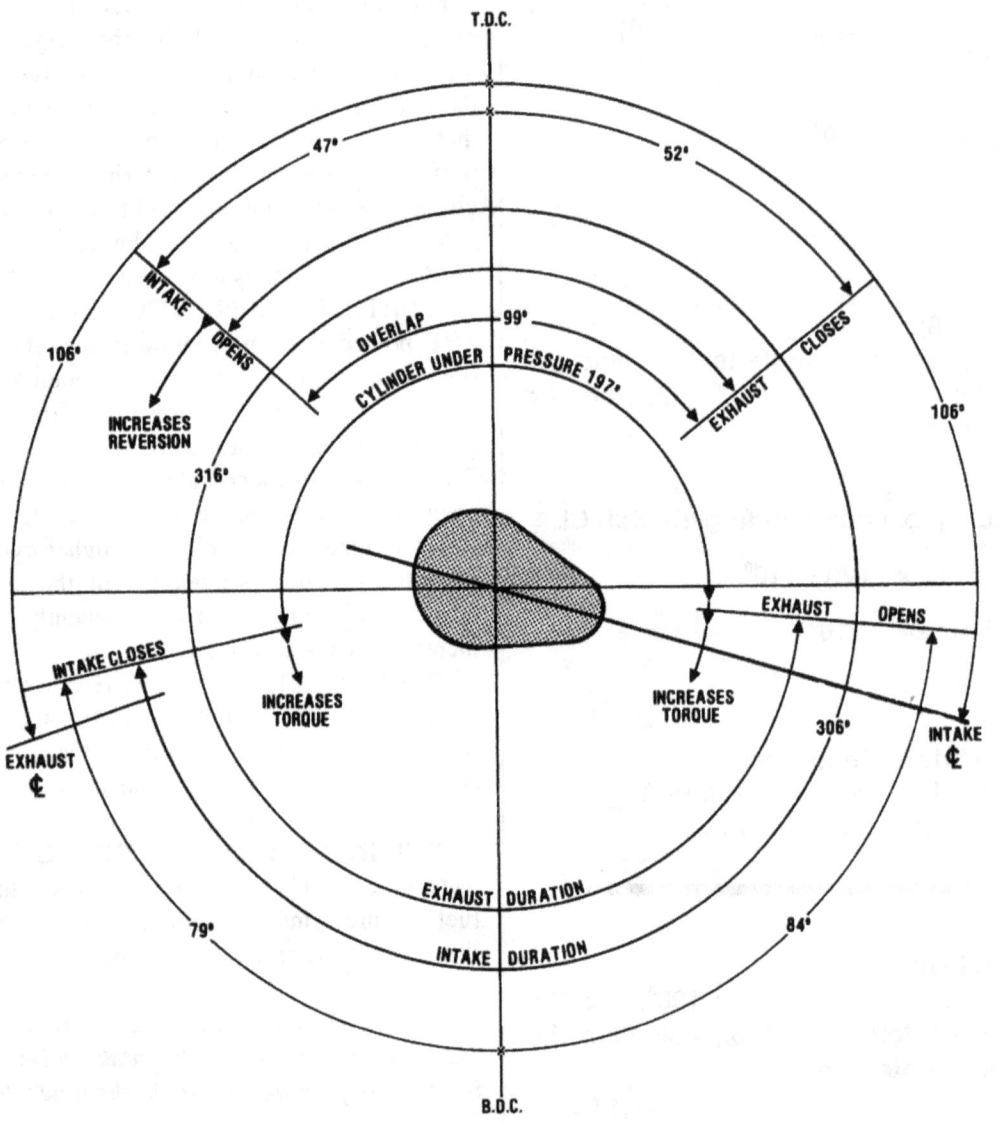

Figure 16f

- The valve timing diagram shown above was reproduced by permission of Competition Cams, Inc.

CHAPTER 17

Carburetor Air Flow

FOR A NORMALLY aspirated engine, induction of the air-fuel mixture into the engine is accomplished by means of the descension of the pistons away from TDC during the intake stroke. This produces a pressure difference between the cylinder and the inlet of the carburetor where atmospheric pressure is existent. Ideally, the air flow rate is a function of engine speed and engine displacement. Although in reality, port contour and roughness, as well as port length, not barring carburetor venturi boosters, throttle plates and choke plates if used(Illustration 17-1), and valve sizes place restrictions on the air flow

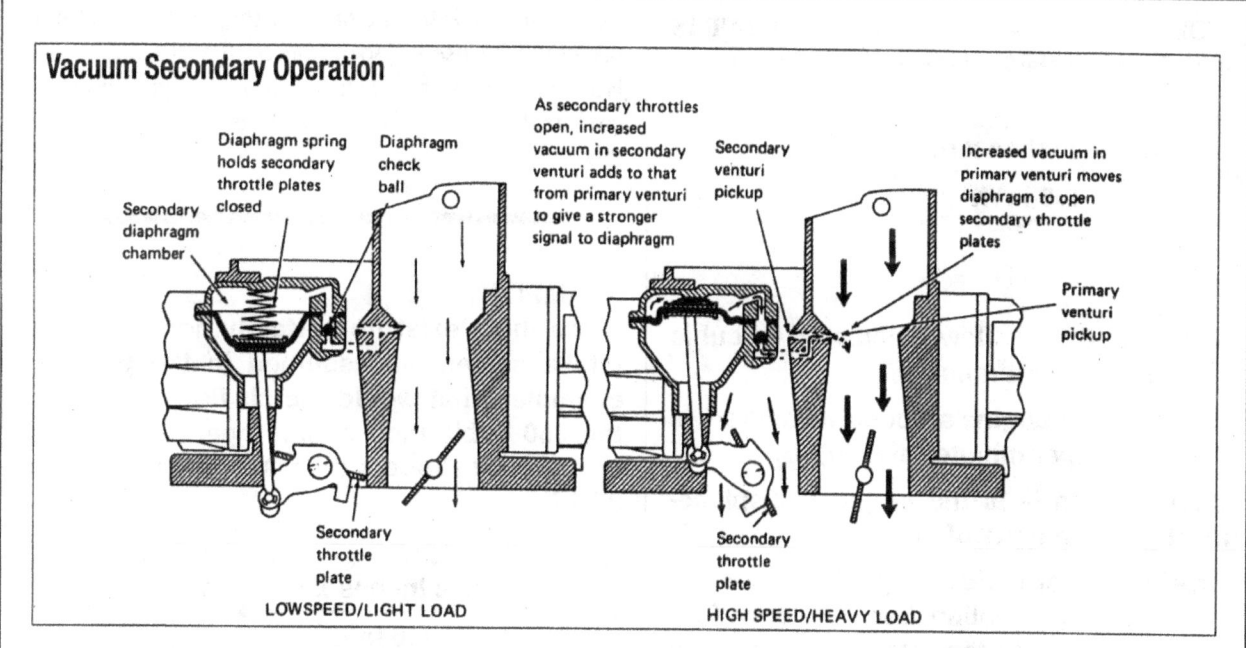

Illustration 17-1: The air flow through the primary venturi at low and high speed has an effect on the air flow through the secondary venturi which has vaccuum operated throttle plates. For our purpose, the air flow will be limited to wide open throttle operation. (Illustration -- Courtesy of Holley Performance)

which in turn affects the engine's mass flow efficiency. So, selection of the adequate or proper size carburetor(s) is a necessity if optimum performance is to be achieved.

CALCULATION OF the engine's air flow potential can be performed through use of the following equations. Since the carburetor(s) air flow rate in cubic feet per minute(CFM) represents the engine's potential air flow capacity it follows that:

IF A **100% air mass efficiency(AME)** is assumed for completely filling the cylinders, the equation will be...

$$CFM = \frac{\text{Cubic Inches} \times \text{rpm}}{2 \times 1728 \text{ in}^3/\text{ft}^3}$$

- or -

$$CFM = \frac{\text{Cubic Inches} \times \text{rpm}}{3456 \text{ in}^3/\text{ft}^3}$$

FOR AN AIR MASS EFFICIENCY THAT IS more or less than **100%**, this equation becomes...

$$CFM = \frac{\text{Cubic Inches} \times \text{rpm}}{3456 \text{ in}^3/\text{ft}^3} \times \frac{\text{AME}}{100}$$

Where,

- CFM -- is the air flow calculated in cubic feet per minute(ft^3/min)
- rpm -- is the engine's speed measured in revolutions per minute(rev/min).
- Cubic Inches -- is the engine's displacement given in units of in^3.
- One-half(1/2 or dividing by 2) was inserted into the first equation because only four pistons complete the intake stroke(for an **8 cylinder engine**) during one revolution of the engine's crankshaft.

- AME -- is the air mass efficiency
- **The conversion factor of "1728 cu inches per cubic foot(1728 in^3/1 ft^3)"** is inserted to convert the cubic inches into cubic feet.

EXAMPLE(17-1):
For an engine having a 350 cubic inch(in^3) displacement, and operating at a peak engine speed of 7000 rpm, what is the maximum carburetor flow rate, assuming ideally, no restriction in the intake system, and 100% air mass efficiency in the cylinders?

$$CFM = \frac{\text{Cubic Inches} \times \text{rpm}}{3456 \text{ in}^3/\text{ft}^3}$$

$$CFM = \frac{350 \text{ in}^3 \times 7000 \text{ rev/min}}{3456 \text{ in}^3/\text{ft}^3}$$

$$CFM = \frac{2450000 \text{ in}^3 \text{ rev/min}}{3456 \text{ in}^3/\text{ft}^3}$$

$$CFM = 708.91 \text{ ft}^3/\text{min}$$

SINCE NO STANDARD carburetors exist for this flow value, a **700 cfm or slightly smaller carburetor** could be used, depending on the engine's usage. However, in another instance, it may require **a larger carburetor flow capacity** such as a **735 cfm or 750 cfm carburetor**.

EXAMPLE(17-2):
Since there exist no perfectly non-restrictive intake system as assumed in the previous example, what would the air flow rate be for the 350 cubic inch engine operating at 7000 rpm if the cylinders air mass efficiency were 85%?

$$CFM = \frac{\text{Cubic Inches} \times \text{rpm}}{3456 \text{ in}^3/\text{ft}^3} \times \frac{\text{AME}}{100}$$

$$CFM = \frac{350 \text{ in}^3 \times 7000 \text{ rev/min}}{3456 \text{ in}^3/\text{ft}^3} \times \frac{85}{100}$$

$$CFM = \frac{2450000 \text{ in}^3/\text{min}}{3456 \text{ in}^3/\text{ft}^3} \times .85$$

$$CFM = 708.91 \text{ ft}^3/\text{min} \times .85$$

$$CFM = 602.57 \text{ ft}^3/\text{min}$$

THEREFORE, a **600 cfm or slightly smaller carburetor** would be adequate, again, depending on its usage. However, in another instance, it may require **a larger carburetor flow capacity** such as a **650 cfm carburetor**.

EXAMPLE(17-3):
What would the air flow rate be for the 350 cubic inch engine operating at 7000 rpm if the cylinders air mass efficiency were 105%?

$$CFM = \frac{\text{Cubic Inches} \times \text{rpm}}{3456 \text{ in}^3/\text{ft}^3} \times \frac{AME}{100}$$

$$CFM = \frac{350 \text{ in}^3 \times 7000 \text{ rev/min}}{3456 \text{ in}^3/\text{ft}^3} \times \frac{105}{100}$$

$$CFM = \frac{2450000 \text{ in}^3/\text{min}}{3456 \text{ in}^3/\text{ft}^3} \times 1.05$$

$$CFM = 708.91 \text{ ft}^3/\text{min} \times 1.05$$

$$CFM = 744.36 \text{ ft}^3/\text{min}$$

THEREFORE, a **750 cfm or slightly smaller carburetor** would be adequate, again, depending on its usage. However, in another instance, it may require **a larger carburetor flow capacity** such as a **780 cfm carburetor**.

EVEN THOUGH THERE IS NO PERFECTLY NON-RESTRICTIVE intake system as stated before in EXAMPLE(17-2), the equation used in EXAMPLE(17-1) can still be used with good results!

CARE SHOULD BE TAKEN WHEN SELECTING A CARBURETOR FOR A vehicle with an automatic transmission. For vehicles with a stock converter, the use of a carburetor with vacuum operated secondaries, instead of mechanical secondaries(for four barrel carburetors) usually works best. If a standard shift transmission is being used, then, it is a matter of choice.

CALCULATIONS

CHAPTER 18

DRIVETRAIN

Overall Gear Ratios

THE OVERALL GEAR RATIO FOR a vehicle's drivetrain is obtained by multiplying the transmission's gear ratios(if a transmission is used) times the rear end gear ratio. Think, what does this mean?

FIRST, LET'S CONSIDER the transmission's gear ratios and then work backwards to the rear end's gear ratio.

(1) If the transmission's 1st gear ratio were 3.27:1, this says the engine or transmission's input shaft will rotate *3.27 revolutions* for every *one revolution* of the transmission's output shaft(or tail shaft).

(2) If the transmission's second gear ratio were 1.98:1, this says the engine or transmission's input shaft will rotate *1.98 revolutions* for every *one revolution* of the transmission's output shaft.

(3) If the transmission's third gear ratio is 1.47:1, this says the engine or transmission's input shaft will rotate *1.47 revolutions* for every *one revolution* of the transmission's output shaft.

(4) For a typical fourth gear ratio of 1.00:1, this says the engine or transmission's input shaft will rotate *1.00 revolution* for every *one revolution* of the transmission's output shaft(the engine's speed and the transmission's output shaft speeds are equal).

(5) Now for fifth gear, this says the engine or transmission's input shaft rotates only *.70 revolutions* for every one revolution of the transmission's output shaft. This condition where the transmission's input shaft or engine turns a less number of times per revolution of the output shaft is known as *overdrive*.

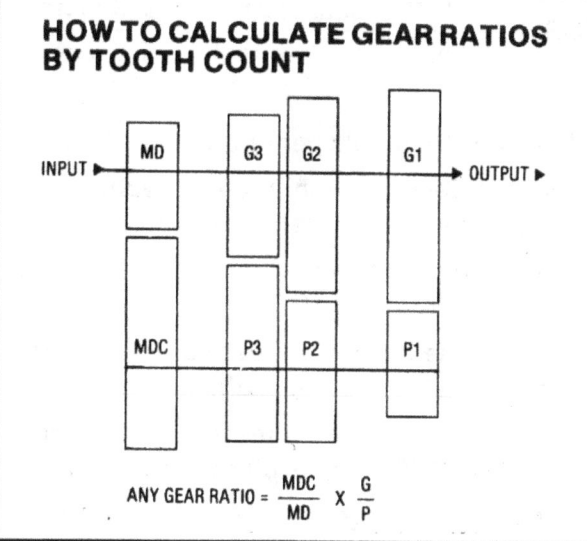

Illustration 18-1: Courtesy of Jerico Performance Products

TO CALCULATE THE transmission's gear ratio for any gear, see Illustration 18-1 and the following: *The rectangles at the top of Illustration 18-1 are the mainshaft gears, and the ones at the bottom are called the cluster shaft gears(also see Figures 18-1 below).*

Top rectangles -- mainshaft gears:

MD -- main drive gear(input shaft gear)
G3 -- third gear
G2 -- second gear
G1-- first gear

Bottom rectangles -- cluster shaft gears:

MDC -- cluster shaft gear that meshes with main drive gear(input shaft gear)
P3 -- cluster shaft gear that meshes with the mainshaft's third gear(G3)
P2 -- cluster shaft gear that meshes with the mainshaft's second gear(G2)
P1-- cluster shaft gear that meshes with the mainshaft's first gear(G1)

$$\text{ANY GEAR RATIO} = \frac{MDC}{MD} \times \frac{G}{P}$$

- OR -

$$TGR = \frac{\text{\# MDC gear teeth}}{\text{\# Input shaft gear teeth}} \times \frac{\text{\# G teeth}}{\text{\# P teeth}}$$

TGR -- transmission's gear ratio in any gear

MDC gear teeth -- the number of teeth on the cluster gear that meshes with MD

Input shaft gear teeth -- the number of teeth on the main drive gear(MD)

G teeth -- the number of teeth on either the G1, G2, or G3 mainshaft gear

P teeth -- the number of teeth on either the P1, P2, or P3 cluster shaft gear

G -- any mainshaft gear such as G1, G2, or G3

G1 -- is first gear on the mainshaft

G2 -- is second gear on the mainshaft
G3 -- is third gear on mainshaft

P -- any cluster shaft gear, such as P1, P2, or P3 that meshes with a mainshaft gear

P1-- the cluster shaft gear that meshes with main shaft gear G1

P2 -- the cluster shaft gear that meshes with main shaft gear G2

P3 -- the cluster shaft gear that meshes with main shaft gear G3

Figure 18-1: You can see from this photograph of a four speed transmission that the mainshaft gears above(from left to right -- MD, G3, G2, and G1) are in <u>constant mesh</u> with the cluster gears below(from left to right -- MDC, P3, P2, and P1) because the mainshaft gears are not splined to the mainshaft that passes through them. So, at any time the clutch is engaged, all of the mainshaft gears and cluster gears are rotating but not all of the mainshaft gears are engaged.
Photograph -- Courtesy of Jerico Performance Products

EXAMPLE(18-1):
For the following 4-speed transmission positioned in <u>first gear</u>:
If the main drive cluster gear(MDC) has 27 teeth, the main drive gear(MD) has 22 teeth, the G1 mainshaft gear has 34 teeth, and the

P1 cluster shaft gear has 15 teeth, calculate the transmission's gear ratio.

$$TGR = \frac{\text{\# MDC gear teeth}}{\text{\# Input shaft gear teeth}} \times \frac{\text{\# G1 teeth}}{\text{\# P1 teeth}}$$

$$TGR = \frac{27 \text{ teeth}}{22 \text{ teeth}} \times \frac{34 \text{ teeth}}{15 \text{ teeth}}$$

$$TGR = 1.227 \times 2.267$$

$$TGR = 2.782$$

THIS CALCULATION CAN BE APPLIED TO **any gear up to third gear** for a **four speed** transmission, but **for fourth gear**, the conventional ratio is **1.000** or "**1 to 1**".

A TABLE OF GEAR TEETH RATIOS, AND TRANSMISSION RATIOS FOR **first**, **second**, **third gear**, and **fourth gear** for *Jerico transmissions* is shown below -- courtesy of Jerico performance products.

FOR THE CASE OF THE rear end gear ratio(ignoring any transmission gear ratios or considering only fourth gear), the same principle applies. This is regarding the rotation of the engine relative to a rear end's ring and pinion gears, or rear axle. If the rear end's gear ratio were 3.50:1, this says that the engine or pinion gear will rotate three and one-half (3.50) times for every single revolution of the ring gear or rear axle(see Figure 18-2).

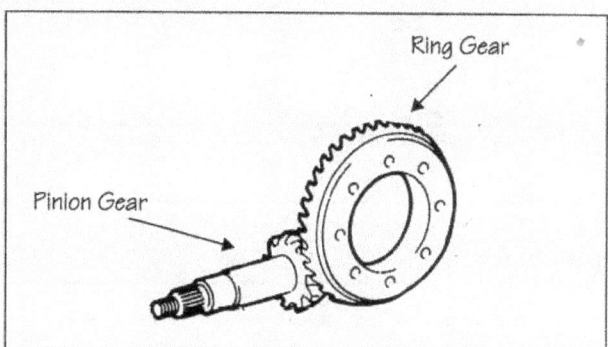

Figure 18-2: Illustration -- Courtesy of Precision Gear

FOR MAIN DRIVE SETS

CLUSTER SHAFT GEAR ÷ INPUT SHIFT GEAR
29/20 EXAMPLE

Main Drive Sets ↓	29/20	28/20	29/21	28/21	27/21	27/22	26/22	26/23	25/23	25/24	24/24	24/25
Main Drive Ratio ↓	1.450	1.400	1.381	1.333	1.286	1.227	1.182	1.130	1.087	1.042	1.000	0.960

MAIN SHAFT GEAR ÷ CLUSTER SHAFT GEAR
34/15 EXAMPLE

FOR SPEED GEARS

Gear	Ratio	29/20	28/20	29/21	28/21	27/21	27/22	26/22	26/23	25/23	25/24	24/24	24/25
1st	34/15	3.287	3.173	3.130	3.022	2.914	2.782	2.679	2.562	2.464	2.361	2.267	2.176
	33/15	3.190	3.080	3.038	2.933	2.829	2.700	2.600	2.487	2.391	2.292	2.200	2.112
	34/16	3.081	2.975	2.935	2.833	2.732	2.608	2.511	2.402	2.310	2.214	2.125	2.040
	33/17	2.815	2.718	2.681	2.588	2.496	2.382	2.294	2.194	2.110	2.022	1.941	1.864
	32/18	2.578	2.489	2.455	2.370	2.286	2.182	2.101	2.010	1.932	1.852	1.778	1.707
	31/18	2.497	2.411	2.378	2.296	2.214	2.114	2.035	1.947	1.872	1.794	1.722	1.653
	32/19	2.442	2.358	2.326	2.246	2.165	2.067	1.990	1.904	1.831	1.754	1.684	1.617
	31/19	2.366	2.284	2.253	2.175	2.098	2.002	1.928	1.844	1.773	1.700	1.632	1.566
	30/20	2.175	2.100	2.071	2.000	1.929	1.841	1.773	1.696	1.630	1.563	1.500	1.440
	30/21	2.071	2.000	1.973	1.905	1.837	1.753	1.688	1.615	1.553	1.488	1.429	1.371
2nd	29/20	2.103	2.030	2.002	1.933	1.864	1.780	1.714	1.639	1.576	1.510	1.450	1.392
	28/20	2.030	1.960	1.933	1.867	1.800	1.718	1.655	1.583	1.522	1.458	1.400	1.344
	29/21	2.002	1.933	1.907	1.841	1.776	1.695	1.632	1.561	1.501	1.438	1.381	1.326
	28/21	1.933	1.867	1.841	1.778	1.714	1.636	1.576	1.507	1.449	1.389	1.333	1.280
	27/21	1.864	1.800	1.776	1.714	1.653	1.578	1.519	1.453	1.398	1.339	1.286	1.234
	27/22	1.780	1.718	1.695	1.636	1.578	1.506	1.450	1.387	1.334	1.278	1.227	1.178
3rd	26/22	1.714	1.655	1.632	1.576	1.519	1.450	1.397	1.336	1.285	1.231	1.182	1.135
	26/23	1.639	1.583	1.561	1.507	1.453	1.387	1.336	1.278	1.229	1.178	1.130	1.085
	25/23	1.576	1.522	1.501	1.449	1.398	1.334	1.285	1.229	1.181	1.132	1.087	1.043
	25/24	1.510	1.458	1.438	1.389	1.339	1.278	1.231	1.178	1.132	1.085	1.042	1.000
	24/24	1.450	1.400	1.381	1.333	1.286	1.227	1.182	1.130	1.087	1.042	1.000	0.960
	24/25	1.392	1.344	1.326	1.280	1.234	1.178	1.135	1.085	1.043	1.000	0.960	0.922
	23/25	1.334	1.288	1.270	1.227	1.183	1.129	1.087	1.040	1.000	0.958	0.920	0.883
	23/26	1.283	1.238	1.222	1.179	1.137	1.086	1.045	1.000	0.962	0.921	0.885	0.849
4th		1 to 1	1 to 1	1 to 1	1 to 1	1 to 1	1 to 1	1 to 1	1 to 1	1 to 1	1 to 1	1 to 1	1 to 1

▪ Special Case Modification Required. NOTE: For 2-Speed Gear Ratio see 3rd Gear. 4th is always 1.1.

CHAPTER EIGHTEEN

THE REAR END GEAR RATIO CAN ALSO BE determined by dividing the number of teeth on the ring gear by the number of teeth on the pinion gear(see Figure 18-2 and TABLE 18-1).

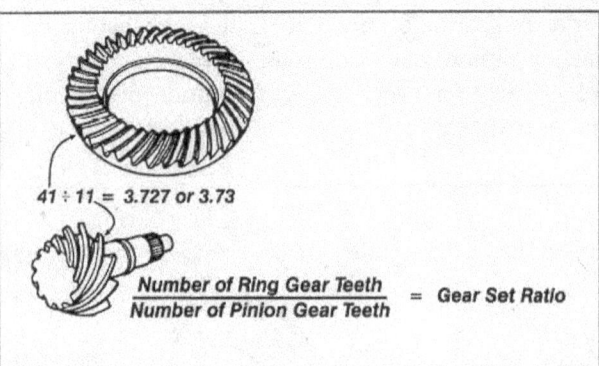

Figure 18-3: Illustration -- Courtesy of Precision Gear

$$REGR = \frac{\text{Number of ring gear teeth}}{\text{Number of pinion gear teeth}}$$

REGR -- rear end gear ratio(same as the "Gear Set Ratio" in Figure 18-2)

EXAMPLE(18-2):
From TABLE 18-1 a ring gear having 37 teeth and a matching pinion gear having 9 teeth (37-9) will yield a rear end gear ratio of...

$$REGR = \frac{\text{Number of ring gear teeth}}{\text{Number of pinion gear teeth}}$$

$$REGR = \frac{37 \text{ teeth}}{9 \text{ teeth}}$$

$$REGR = 4.11$$

NOW, BACK TO THE *overall gear ratio!* If you multiply the transmission's gear ratio(first, second, third, fourth, fifth or sixth gear in some cases) times the rear end's gear ratio, the results would be an overall gear ratio. This says the product of these two

Street Gear

Ratio	Teeth	Part No.	
2.80	42-15	49-0107-1	
2.86	40-14	49-0106-1	
2.91	32-11	49-0121-1	New
2.94	47-16	49-0105-1	
3.00	39-13	49-0038-1	
3.07	43-14	49-0092-1	
3.25	39-12	69-0284-1	
3.33	40-12	69-0266-1	New
3.40	34-10	69-0364-1	New
3.45	38-11	69-0414-1	New
3.50	35-10	49-0027-1	
3.55	39-11	69-0195-1	
3.60	36-10	69-0365-1	
3.70	37-10	69-0361-1	
3.75	45-12	69-0366-1	
3.82	42-11	69-0286-1	
3.89	35-9	69-0177-1	
4.00	36-9	69-0272-1	
4.11	37-9	69-0179-1	
4.22	38-9	69-0367-1	
4.33	39-9	69-0161-1	
4.44	40-9	69-0368-1	
4.50	36-8	69-0369-1	
4.56	41-9	69-0185-1	
4.63	37-8	69-0379-1	
4.71	33-7	69-0362-1	
4.86	34-7	69-0067-1	
5.00	35-7	69-0360-1	
5.14	36-7	69-0068-1	
5.29	37-7	69-0270-1	
5.43	38-7	69-0069-1	
5.50	33-6	69-0363-1	New
5.67	34-6	69-0070-1	
5.83	35-6	69-0288-1	
6.00	36-6	69-0199-1	
6.20	31-5	69-0290-1	
6.33	38-6	69-0276-1	
6.50	39-6	69-0197-1	

TABLE 18-1: The data above shows some gear ratios for a 9" rear end and the corresponding number of teeth on the ring and pinion gears.
Table -- By Permission of Richmond Gear

ratios would be the same as having a single gear ratio of the same value.

THE EQUATION FOR CALCULATING THIS value is given below, followed by an example.

Overall Gear Ratio(G) = TGR x REGR

Where,

G -- any mainshaft(transmission) gear

TGR -- Transmission Gear Ratio

REGR -- Rear End Gear Ratio

EXAMPLE(18-3):
For the following transmission gear ratios, and rear end gear ratio, calculate the overall gear ratio for each transmission gear.

Given: Transmission Gear Ratios -- TGR(G)
TGR(1st) = 3.27:1
TGR(2nd) = 1.98:1
TGR(3rd) = 1.47:1
TGR(4th) = 1.00:1
TGR(5th) = 0.70:1

Rear End Gear Ratio(REGR) = 3.50:1

Overall Gear Ratio(G) = TGR x REGR

Overall Gear Ratio(1st) = 3.27 x 3.50 = 11.445:1

Overall Gear Ratio(2nd) = 1.98 x 3.50 = 6.93:1

Overall Gear Ratio(3rd) = 1.47 x 3.50 = 5.145:1

Overall Gear Ratio(4th) = 1.00 x 3.50 = 3.50:1

Overall Gear Ratio(5th) = 0.70 x 3.50 = 2.45:1

Notice, for first gear the product of these two ratios yields an **overall ratio of 11.445:1**, which says that the same thing would be accomplished if a ratio of this proportion is used as opposed to the product of the other **two ratios(3.27 x 3.50)**. This says that the **engine rotates 11.445 times** to every **one revolution of the rear axle**. The same principle applies to all of the other remaining overall gear ratios.

CALCULATIONS

CHAPTER 19

TRANSMISSION

Output Shaft Speed

THE SPEED OF THE transmission's output shaft (see Figure 19-1) is determined by simply dividing the engine speed by the transmission's gear ratio (any gear that it is currently in). You might ask, what is the purpose or significance of knowing the transmission's output shaft speed?. Well, it can be applied in determining the amount of clutch slippage when using a standard shift transmission. For an automatic transmission it can be used to detect any amount of slippage resulting from the bands being worn, and/or clutch slippage, and slippage in the torque converter. Also, the output shaft speed in conjunction with the rear axle ratio helps determine the rear axle speed, which influences the vehicle's speed depending on the tire's diameter or rolling radius.

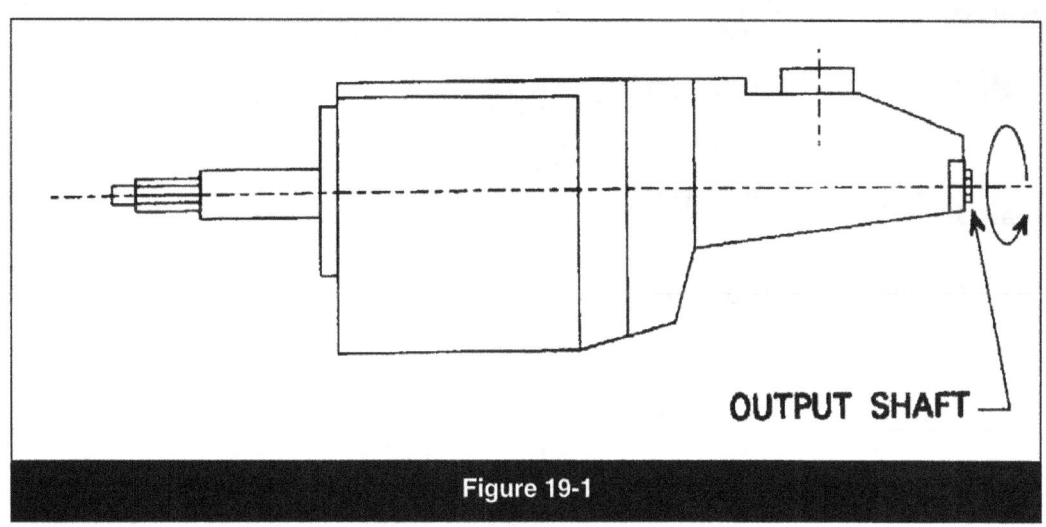

Figure 19-1

$$\boxed{\text{Output Shaft Speed(G)} = \frac{\text{Engine Speed(rpm)}}{\text{TGR}}}$$

Output Shaft Speed(G) -- The transmission's output shaft speed in any gear

TGR -- Transmission Gear Ratio

G -- any gear that the transmission is in

EXAMPLE(19):
For an engine speed of 6000 rpm and for the following transmission gear ratios that were given in Chapter 18, what are the corresponding transmission output speeds?

Given:
TGR(1st) = 3.27:1
TGR(2nd) = 1.98:1
TGR(3rd) = 1.47:1
TGR(4th) = 1.00:1
TGR(5th) = 0.70:1

$$\boxed{\text{Output Shaft Speed(G)} = \frac{\text{Engine Speed(rpm)}}{\text{TGR}}}$$

Output Shaft Speed(1st) = $\dfrac{6000 \text{ rpm}}{3.27}$

Output Shaft Speed(1st) = 1834.86 rpm

Output Shaft Speed(2nd) = $\dfrac{6000 \text{ rpm}}{1.98}$

Output Shaft Speed(2nd) = 3030.30 rpm

Output Shaft Speed(3rd) = $\dfrac{6000 \text{ rpm}}{1.47}$

Output Shaft Speed(3rd) = 4081.63 rpm

Output Shaft Speed(4th) = $\dfrac{6000 \text{ rpm}}{1.00}$

Output Shaft Speed(4th) = 6000 rpm

Output Shaft Speed(5th) = $\dfrac{6000 \text{ rpm}}{0.70}$

Output Shaft Speed(5th) = 8571.43 rpm

CHAPTER 20

REAR END

Axle Speed

THE REAR END'S AXLE *speed* is a function of the engine speed(see Figure 20-1), transmission gear ratio(if a transmission is used), and the rear end's gear ratio. Stated otherwise, it is a function of the engine speed and overall gear ratio. That means the engine speed divided by the overall gear ratio equals the rear axle speed. An essential purpose of knowing the rear axle speed is to help determine the vehicle's maximum speed when the tire diameter or loaded tire radius is known.

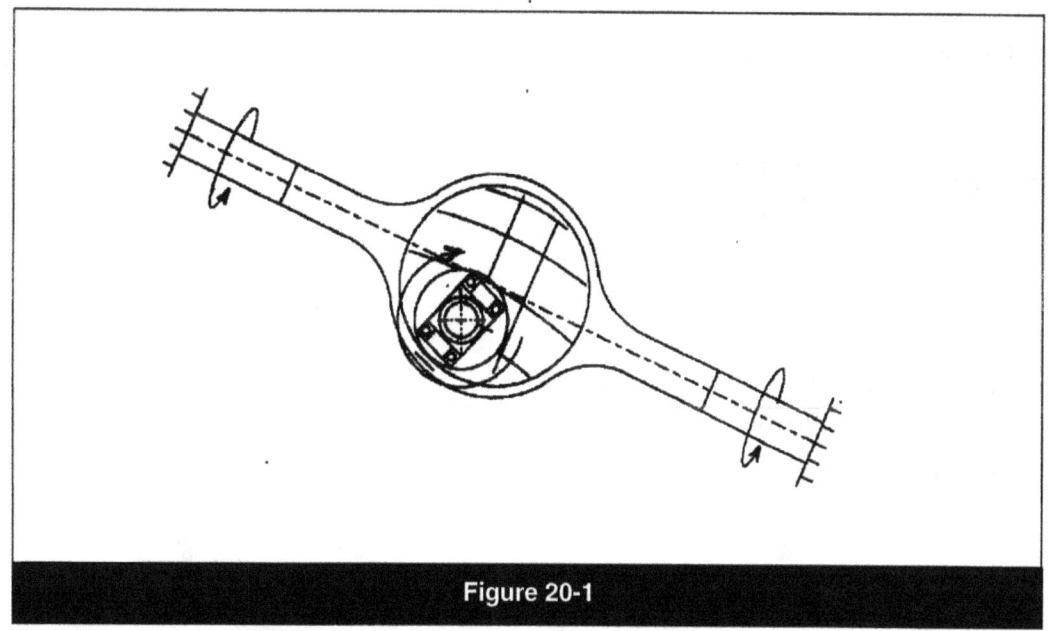

Figure 20-1

$$\text{Rear Axle Speed(G)} = \frac{\text{Engine Speed(rpm)}}{\text{Overall Gear Ratio(G)}}$$

Rear Axle Speed(G) = The rear end's ratio in any gear

Overall Gear Ratio(G) -- The overall gear ratio in any gear

EXAMPLE(20):
For an engine speed of 6000 rpm and the following overall gear ratios from Chapter 18, the rear axle speed will be...

Given:

Overall Gear Ratio(1st) = 11.445:1

Overall Gear Ratio(2nd) = 6.93:1

Overall Gear Ratio(3rd) = 5.145:1

Overall Gear Ratio(4th) = 3.50:1

Overall Gear Ratio(5th) = 2.45:1

$$\text{Rear Axle Speed(G)} = \frac{\text{Engine Speed(rpm)}}{\text{Overall Gear Ratio(G)}}$$

$$\text{Rear Axle Speed}(1^{st}) = \frac{6000 \text{ rpm}}{11.445}$$

Rear Axle Speed(1st) = 524.246 rpm

$$\text{Rear Axle Speed}(2^{nd}) = \frac{6000 \text{ rpm}}{6.93}$$

Rear Axle Speed(2nd) = 865.80 rpm

$$\text{Rear Axle Speed}(3^{rd}) = \frac{6000 \text{ rpm}}{5.145}$$

Rear Axle Speed(3rd) = 1166.18 rpm

$$\text{Rear Axle Speed}(4^{th}) = \frac{6000 \text{ rpm}}{3.50}$$

Rear Axle Speed(4th) = 1714.29 rpm

$$\text{Rear Axle Speed}(5^{th}) = \frac{6000 \text{ rpm}}{2.45}$$

Rear Axle Speed(5th) = 2448.98 rpm

CHAPTER 21

MAXIMUM VEHICLE SPEED

AS A FUNCTION OF THE:

- **ENGINE SPEED(RPM)**
- **STATIC LOADED TIRE RADIUS**
- **TRANSMISSION GEAR RATIO(TGR)**
- **AND REAR END GEAR RATIO(REGR)**

QUESTIONS MAY often arise about the optimum obtainable speed that one's vehicle(automobile) can achieve when the transmission is in either first, second, third, fourth, fifth, or sixth gear.

BUT FIRST, LET'S DEFINE speed. *Speed is the change in distance with respect to time or the amount of distance covered divided by the time taken to travel that distance.*

JUST HOW LONG IT will take to get to the maximum speed is affected by how much horsepower and torque is produced by the engine, tire size, tire traction rating or tire compound, vehicle weight, gear ratios, track or road surface, atmospheric conditions, suspension, etc.

SOMETHING TO NOTE ABOUT the tire's size(once it has been selected) is that, when it is placed on the vehicle, the weight of the vehicle will compress the tire to some degree. The amount of compression will depend predominantly upon the vehicle's weight, and tire pressure. This compression

> ...there will be an increase in tire growth as the vehicle is accelerated, which will in turn increase the loaded tire radius because of the centrifugal force resulting from the increase in speed ...

Figure 20-1: Under acceleration the rear tires will become compressed to some degree due to the car's weight transfer and the torque applied by the tires on the road, this results in a decrease in the loaded tire radius; but, as the engine speed increases in a particular gear the tire speed increases causing the rear tires to grow which results is an increase in the loaded tire radius.
Photo -- Courtesy of Pontiac Racing.

will affect the static loaded tire radius between the road or ground and the center of the wheel. Consider also that there will be an increase in tire growth as the vehicle is accelerated, which will in turn increase the loaded tire radius because of the centrifugal force resulting from the increase in speed thereof. A tire's growth will also be limited by its construction(number and type of plys, etc.).

THE STATIC LOADED TIRE RADIUS is determined by measurement when all tires are not rotating, and are planted(by the vehicle & driver's weight) on a hard surface.

(If a tire is inflated to the proper air pressure- and it is not very flate at the road's surface, the static loaded radius can be estimated by the following equation. However, If it is very flat at the road's surface, the static loaded tire radius will have to be measured from the road to center of the wheel.)

$$\text{SLTR} = \frac{\text{Tire Diameter(in)}}{2}$$

SLTR -- Static Loaded Tire Radius(in)

$$\text{Tire Circumference} = 6.2832 \times \text{SLTR(in)}$$

$$\text{Tire Rev/Mile} = \frac{10084.034 \text{ rev/mile}}{\text{SLTR(in)}}$$

Tire Rev/Mile -- the number of tire revolutions per mile or how many times a tire will rotate in a distance of one mile

$$\text{Max Speed(G)} = \frac{\text{Engine Speed} \times 60 \text{ min/hr}}{\text{TGR} \times \text{REGR} \times \text{Tire Rev/Mile}}$$

Max Speed(G) -- the maximum vehicle speed in any gear

Engine Speed -- engine rpm

EXAMPLE(21):
For an engine speed of 6000 rpm and tire diameter of 29 inches along with the following transmission gear ratios and rear end gear ratio from Chapter 18, the maximum vehicle

speed for each transmission gear ratio will be...

Given:
$TGR(1^{st}) = 3.27:1$
$TGR(2^{nd}) = 1.98:1$
$TGR(3^{rd}) = 1.47:1$
$TGR(4^{th}) = 1.00:1$
$TGR(5^{th}) = 0.70:1$
Rear end gear ratio = 3.50:1

$$SLTR = \frac{\text{Tire Diameter(in)}}{2}$$

$$SLTR = \frac{29"}{2}$$

$$SLTR = 14.5"$$

$$\text{Tire Rev/Mile} = \frac{10084.034 \text{ Rev/Mile}}{SLTR(in)}$$

$$\text{Tire Rev/Mile} = \frac{10084.034 \text{ Rev/Mile}}{14.5"}$$

Tire Rev/Mile = 695.451 Rev/Mile

So,

$$\text{Max Speed}(1^{st}) = \frac{6000 \text{ Rev/Min} \times 60 \text{ Min/hr}}{3.27 \times 3.50 \times 695.451 \text{ Rev/Mile}}$$

$$\text{Max Speed}(1^{st}) = \frac{360000 \text{ Rev/hr}}{11.445 \times 695.451 \text{ Rev/Mile}}$$

$$\text{Max Speed}(1^{st}) = \frac{360000 \text{ Rev/hr}}{7959.44 \text{ Rev/Mile}}$$

Max Speed(1st) = 45.229 Miles/hr

Therefore,

$$\text{Max Speed}(2^{nd}) = \frac{6000 \text{ Rev/Min} \times 60 \text{ Min/hr}}{1.98 \times 3.50 \times 695.451 \text{ Rev/Mile}}$$

$$\text{Max Speed}(2^{nd}) = \frac{360000 \text{ Rev/hr}}{6.93 \times 695.451 \text{ Rev/Mile}}$$

$$\text{Max Speed}(2^{nd}) = \frac{360000 \text{ Rev/hr}}{4819.475 \text{ Rev/Mile}}$$

Max Speed(2nd) = 74.697 Miles/hr

$$\text{Max Speed}(3^{rd}) = \frac{6000 \text{ Rev/Min} \times 60 \text{ Min/hr}}{1.47 \times 3.50 \times 695.451 \text{ Rev/Mile}}$$

$$\text{Max Speed}(3^{rd}) = \frac{360000 \text{ Rev/hr}}{5.145 \times 695.451 \text{ Rev/Mile}}$$

$$\text{Max Speed}(3^{rd}) = \frac{360000 \text{ Rev/hr}}{3578.095 \text{ Rev/Mile}}$$

Max Speed(3rd) = 100.612 Miles/hr

$$\text{Max Speed}(4^{th}) = \frac{6000 \text{ Rev/Min} \times 60 \text{ Min/hr}}{1.00 \times 3.50 \times 695.451 \text{ Rev/Mile}}$$

$$\text{Max Speed}(4^{th}) = \frac{360000 \text{ Rev/hr}}{3.50 \times 695.451 \text{ Rev/Mile}}$$

$$\text{Max Speed}(4^{th}) = \frac{360000 \text{ Rev/hr}}{2434.079 \text{ Rev/Mile}}$$

Max Speed(4th) = 147.90 Miles/hr

$$\text{Max Speed}(5^{th}) = \frac{6000 \text{ Rev/Min} \times 60 \text{ Min/hr}}{0.70 \times 3.50 \times 695.451 \text{ Rev/Mile}}$$

$$\text{Max Speed}(5^{th}) = \frac{360000 \text{ Rev/hr}}{2.45 \times 695.451 \text{ Rev/Mile}}$$

$$\text{Max Speed}(5^{th}) = \frac{360000 \text{ Rev/hr}}{1703.855 \text{ Rev/Mile}}$$

Max Speed(5th) = 211.286 Miles/hr

THE LOADED RADIUS IS referred to when the vehicle is set in motion.

THE STATIC LOADED radius in the previous examples was taken equal to one-half(1/2) of the tire's diameter for simplicity. Although, in reality the static loaded radius is moderately less than one-half of the diameter.

REMEMBER THAT THE LOADED RADIUS WILL increase as the tire's rpm or axle speed increases. This will cause an increase in the maximum vehicle speed as compared to the maximum vehicle speed calculated using the static loaded tire radius. Again, the actual static loaded radius can be measured while the vehicle is sitting still.

THE EQUATION FOR THE "**Tire circumference**" on page 114 was added <u>only</u> for those who would like to calculate the distance around the outer surface of a tire with or without tread.

- **NOTE:** *If a transmission is not used, the transmission's gear ratio in the "Max Speed(G)" equation should be taken as 1.00:1 or 1.00, because the use of a direct drive(drive shaft) between the clutch and rear end would be the same as having a transmission with a 1.00:1 high gear ratio.*

ABBREVIATIONS

ANGLES

- a -- alpha -- crankshaft angle of rotation; rod angularity
- deg -- degree(s)
- (°) -- deg or degrees
- Functions of the crank angle alpha(α): a,b,c,d
- rad -- radian(s)
- Rev, rev -- revolution(s)

AREA

- Cyl Area -- cylinder area
- ft^2 -- (square foot - or - square feet)
- in^2 -- square inch(es)

CONSTANTS

- Ideal gas constant(for air) -- 53.34 ft-lbf / lbm-°R
- p(PI - or - pi) -- 3.14159
- Z -- the number of revolutions necessary to complete one cycle of engine operation, Z=2 for four stroke engine

---

DISTANCE / LENGTH

- c -- piston pin height
- C -- circumference of a circle
- Dk Ht -- Deck Height
- D -- Dk Ht Clearance
- D, d -- diameter of a circle
- ft -- (foot - or - feet)
- (') -- (foot - or - feet)
- in -- inch(es)
- (") -- inch(es)
- Mi, mi -- mile
- PD -- piston displacement(in inches)
- r -- crank throw(in inches)
- R -- rod length(in inches)
- SLTR -- static loaded tire radius

EFFICIENCY

- AME -- air mass efficiency
- Air Mass Eff(carb) -- air mass efficiency as a function of the carburetor's flow rate
- Air Mass Eff(% reduc) -- the percent reduction in air mass efficiency
- Air Mass Eff(rpm) -- air mass efficiency as a function of the carburetor and engine speed(RPM, rpm) ratings
- Net AME -- net air mass efficiency
- Net Air Mass Eff(carb) -- the net air mass efficiency as a result of "air mass eff(carb)"
- NetAir Mass Eff(rpm) -- the net air mass efficiency as a result of "air mass eff(rpm)"
- % AME -- the percent air mass efficiency

FLOW RATE(S)

- CFM, cfm -- ft^3/min -- cubic feet per minute

ABBREVIATIONS

FORCE

- F_H -- horizontal force component
- F_P -- perpendicular force component

- lb -- pound force or pound weight
- lbf -- pound force
- lbs -- pounds of force or pounds of weight

GEARS

- G -- any mainshaft gear
- MD -- mainshaft gear
- MDC -- is the cluster gear that meshes with the main drive gear
- #G teeth -- the number of teeth on any mainshaft gear
- #P teeth -- the number of teeth on any cluster shaft gear
- P -- any cluster shaft gear
- REGR -- rear end gear ratio
- TGR -- transmission gear ratio

MASS

- Air Mass Eff -- Air Mass Efficiency
- Act Air Mass -- actual air mass
- lbm -- pound mass
- Theo Air Mass -- theoretical air mass

PERFORMANCE FACTORS

- Static C.R. -- static compression ratio
- Dynamic C.R. -- dynamic compression ratio

POWER

- Bhp, bhp -- brake horsepower
- HP, hp -- horsepower

PRESSURE

- AP -- partial pressure due to the air
- ATM, Atm, atm, -- atmospheric
- Atm Pres -- atmospheric pressure
- Baro Pres -- barometric pressure
- BMEP, bmep -- brake mean effective pressure
- FMEP, fmep -- friction mean effective pressure
- GP -- saturation pressure
- IMEP, imep -- indicated mean effective pressure
- in-hg -- inches of mercury
- MEP, mep -- mean effective pressure
- psi -- lbf/in^2, gauge
- psia -- pounds per square inch, absolute
- VP -- vapor pressure

QUANTITIES

- n -- number of cylinders
- No. Of Cyl -- number of cylinders

ABBREVIATIONS

ROTATION
- ccw -- counter clockwise ↑
- cw -- clockwise ↓
- Deg, deg -- degree(s)
- Rev, rev -- revolution(s)

- Z -- the number of revolutions that are necessary to complete one power stroke per piston

----

SPEED / VELOCITY / ACCELERATION
- Avg -- average
- Avg Piston Speed -- average piston speed
- Crankpin Angular Veloc -- crankpin angular velocity(radians/min - or - radians per minute - or - rad/min)
- Crankpin Veloc -- crankpin velocity
- ft/min -- feet per minute(fpm)
- ft/sec -- feet per second(fps)
- in/min -- inches per minute(ipm)
- in/sec -- inches per second(ips)
- IPS -- instantaneous piston speed
- MPH, mph -- miles/hour - or - mi/hr
- N -- engine speed(rpm)
- No. of Crank Revolutions -- number of crankshaft revolutions
- Rev/Mi, rev/mi -- revolutions/mile
- RPM, rpm -- rev/min -- revolutions per minute
- RPS, rps -- rev/sec -- revolutions per second
- Tire Rev/Mile -- tire revolutions per mile

SYMBOLS
- (-) -- negative
- (+) -- positive

TEMPERATURE
- Atm Temp -- atmospheric temperature
- °F -- degrees Fahrenheit
- °R -- degrees Rankine
- Temp -- Temperature

TIME
- Hr, hr -- hour(s)
- Min, min -- minute(s)
- Sec, sec -- second(s)
- Sec/Min, sec/min -- seconds per minute

TORQUE / WORK
- ft-lbf -- [(foot-pound force) - or - (foot-pound)]
- lbf-ft -- [(pound force-feet) - or - (pound-feet)]

VALVE TIMING
- ABDC -- intake valve closing time <u>after bottom dead center</u>
- ATDC -- exhaust valve closing time <u>after top dead center</u>

ABBREVIATIONS

- BBDC -- exhaust valve opening time <u>before bottom dead center</u>
- BDC -- bottom dead center
- BTDC -- intake valve opening time <u>before top dead center</u>
- EC -- exhaust valve closing point(time)
- EO -- exhaust valve opening point(time)
- Exh CL -- exhaust lobe center line
- IC -- intake valve closing point(time)
- Intake CL -- intake lobe center line
- IO -- intake valve opening point(time)
- Lobe Sep Angle -- Lobe separation angle
- TDC -- top dead center

VOLUME

- cc -- cubic centimeters
- ccv -- combustion chamber volume per cylinder
- cu in -- cubic inch(es)
- Cyl Volume -- cylinder volume
- Cylinder Vol -- cylinder volume
- dcv -- deck height clearance volume per cylinder
- dsv -- dynamic swept volume
- Engine Displ -- engine displacement
- hgv -- compressed head gasket volume per cylinder
- in^3 -- cubic inch(es)
- pdv -- piston dome or dish volume per cylinder
- sv -- swept volume
- Total Eng Displ -- total engine displacement

WEIGHT

- lb -- pound
- lbs -- pounds

OTHERS

- Carb -- carburetor(S)
- Cyl -- cylinder(s)
- reduc -- reduction

CONVERSIONS

ANGLES
- 1 deg = 0.01745 rad
- 360 deg = 6.282 rad
- No. of degrees = No. of radians / 0.01745
- π(pi) = 3.14159 rad
- π(pi) = 180°
- $\pi/4$ = 0.7854
- 2π = 6.28318 rad
- 2π = 360°
- 1 rad = 57.296 deg
- 1 rad = 3437.7468 min
- No. of radians = No. of degrees x 0.01745
- 1 rev = 360°

AREA
- $1\ cm^2$ = 0.155 in^2
- $1\ ft^2$ = 929.0304 cm^2
- $1\ ft^2$ = 144 in^2
- $1\ in^2$ = 6.45161 cm^2
- $1\ in^2$ = 0.000579 ft^2
- $1\ in^2$ = 645.16 mm^2

DISTANCE / LENGTH
- 1 cm = 0.3937 in
- 1 cm = 393.70079 mils
- 1 ft = 30.48 cm
- 1 ft = 12 in
- No. of feet = No. of inches / 12 inches
- 1 in = 2.54 cm
- 1 in = 0.083 ft
- 1 in = 1000 mils
- 1 in = 25.4 mm
- 1 mi = 5280 ft
- No. miles = No. of feet / 5280 ft
- 1 mil = 0.00254 cm
- 1 mil = 0.0000833 feet
- 1 mil = 0.001 in
- 1 millimeter = 0.1 cm
- 1 millimeter = 0.03937 inches
- 1 millimeter = 39.37 mils

ENERGY / WORK
- 1 ft-lbf = 12 in-lbf
- 1 lbf-ft = 12 lbf-in

POWER
- 1 hp = 33000 ft-lbf/min
- 1 hp = 550 ft-lbf/sec
- 550 ft-lbf/sec = 33000 ft-lbf/min

PRESSURE
- 1 atm = 29.92 in-Hg
- 1 atm = 407.10 in-H_2O
- 1 atm = 14.7 lbf/in^2
- 1 in-Hg = 13.60628 in-H_2O
- 1 in-Hg = 0.49118 lbf/in^2
- 1 in-H_2O = 0.07349 in-Hg
- 1 lbf/in^2 = 2.03593 in-Hg
- 1 lbf/in^2 = 27.70083 in-H_2O
- 0.49118 lbf/in^2 / (in-Hg)
- 0.03601 lbf/in^2 / (in-H_2O)
- 14.696 lbf/in^2 = 29.92 in-Hg
- 14.696 lbf/in^2 = 407.10 in-H_2O

SPEED / VELOCITY
- 1 cm/sec = 0.03281 ft/sec
- 1 cm/sec = 0.3937 in/sec
- 1 ft/min = .01667 ft/sec
- 1 ft/sec = 30.48 cm/sec
- 1 ft/sec = 12 in/sec
- 1 g = 32.174 ft/sec^2
- 1 g = 21.937 (mi/hr)/sec
- 1 in/min = .01667 in/sec
- 1 in/sec = 2.54 cm/sec
- 1 in/sec = 0.08333 ft/sec
- 1 mph = 88 ft/min
- 1 mph = 1.46667 ft/sec
- 1 rad/min = 0.01667 rad/sec
- 1 rev/min = 0.01667 rev/sec
- No. of rev/sec = No. of rpm / 60
  = No. of rev/min / 60

CONVERSIONS

TEMPERATURE
- °F = °R - 459.67
- °R = 459.67 + °F

TIME
- 1hr = 60 min
- 1 min = 60 sec

VOLUME
- 1 cm^3(cc) = 0.06102 in^3
- 1 cm^3(cc) = 0.001 liters
- 1 ft^3 = 1728 in^3
- 1 in^3 = 16.387 cm^3 - or - 16.387 cc
- 1 in^3 = 0.01638 liters
- 1 liter = 1000 cm^3(cc)
- 1 liter = 61.04651 in^3
- 1 milliliter = 1 cm^3(cc)
- 1 milliliter = 0.001 liter

WEIGHT
- 1 gram = .00221 lbs
- 1 gram = 0.03527 oz
- 1 lb = 453.592 grams
- 1 lb = 16 oz
- 1 oz = 28.3495 grams
- 1 oz = 0.0625 lbs

OTHER(S)
- % / 100 = a decimal number

GLOSSARY

Absolute pressure -- This is equal to the atmospheric pressure plus or minus any gage pressure.

Actual air mass -- This is the actual mass of air taken into the cylinder.

After bottom dead center(ABDC) -- This is when the piston is moving away from BDC on the compression or exhaust stroke.

After top dead center(ATDC) -- This is when the piston is moving away from TDC on the intake or power stroke.

Air mass efficiency(AME) -- It is the ratio of the actual mass of air taken into the cylinder to the theoretical mass of air that could be inducted into the cylinder.

% Air mass efficiency(% AME) -- This is the air mass efficiency multiplied times 100.

Ambient pressure -- It is the atmospheric or surrounding environmental pressure exerted by the air and water-vapor in the air.

Ambient temperature -- It is the atmospheric or surrounding environmental temperature.

Atmospheric pressure -- see "ambient pressure"

Atmospheric pressure(standard) -- It is an exerted pressure of one atmosphere (1atm), which is equal to 14.696 lbf/in^2 .

Atmospheric temperature -- see "ambient temperature"

Average force -- This is the sum of all forces applied on an object divided by the total number of forces*[Example: (100 lbs + 50 lbs + 200 lbs + 150 lbs) / 4 = 125 lbs]*.

Average Piston Speed -- The total distance traveled by the piston during one complete one revolution of the crankshaft times the engine speed(in rpm's).

Barometric pressure -- It is the atmospheric pressure that is measured by a barometer.

Before bottom dead center(BBDC) -- This is when the piston is approaching BDC on the intake or power stroke.

Before top dead center(BTDC) -- This is when the piston is approaching TDC on the compression or exhaust stroke.

Bore -- This is the diameter of an engine's cylinders.

Bottom dead center(BDC) -- This is when the piston has reached its lowest point in the cylinder.

GLOSSARY

Brake mean effective pressure -- The indicated mean effective pressure minus the friction mean pressure, and other mean effective pressure losses due to the compression process, etc.

Brake torque -- The indicated torque minus the frictional torque necessary to overcome friction and any other losses due to the compression stroke and, etc.

Compression phase -- The is the time(measured in degrees) *during the compression stroke* when the intake valve closes, until the time(measured in degrees) *during this same compression stroke* when ignition of the air-fuel mixture takes place.

Compression stroke -- This is when compression of the air-fuel mixture takes place as the piston moves from BDC to TDC while both the intake and exhaust valves are closed.

Constant force -- A continous applied force that remains the same.

Crank throw(r) -- It is one half of the crankshaft's stroke.

Cylinder pressure -- This is the amount of force exerted on top of the piston divided by the cylinder area. Also, the pressure exerted by the burning air-fuel mixture and compression of the air-fuel mixture charge.

Deceleration -- This is a decrease in speed over some span of time.

Degrees Fahrenheit(°F) -- This is equal to *degrees rankine* minus *460 degrees*.

Degrees Rankine(°R) -- This is equal to *degrees fahrenheit* plus *460 degrees*.

Deck Height(Dk Ht) -- The distance from the centerline of the crankshaft to the crown of the cylinder block.

Diameter -- The distance or length of a straight line passing from one side of a circle or cylinder bore through its center to the other side.

Distance -- The amount of space between two points measured along a line or curve, or both.

Drivetrain -- It is composed of the transmission, drive shaft, and rear end(in this case, for rear wheel driven vehicles).

Dry bulb temperature -- This is the actual atmospheric temperature measurement as indicated by a plain thermometer.

Duration -- This is the length of time(in degrees) that the intake or exhaust valve remains open during one cycle of engine operation.

GLOSSARY

Dynamic compression ratio -- This is the volume calculated above the piston at the point when the intake valve has completely closed, during the compression stroke, to the volume above the piston when it is at top dead center.

Engine displacement -- This is the volume that remains above the piston after it travels from top dead center to bottom dead center(through one stroke of the crankshaft), times the number of cylinders.

Engine torque -- The twisting or rotational turning moment about a point, such as a crankshaft being caused to rotate about the center of its main journals.

Engine horsepower -- This is the engine's work output per minute or second divided by the unit of one horsepower which is ***33,000 foot-pounds per minute(ft-lbs/min)*** -- or -- ***550 foot-pounds per second(ft-lbs/sec)***. This value is a dimensionless number.

Exhaust closing time(E C) -- This is the time(in degrees) when the exhaust valve closes at the end of the exhaust phase(during the intake stroke).

Exhaust lobe centerline(Exhaust CL) -- This is the angle at which maximum valve lift occurs on the exhaust lobe.

Exhaust opening time(E O) -- This is the time(in degrees) when the exhaust valve opens at the beginning of the exhaust phase(during the power stroke).

Exhaust phase -- This is the time(measured in degrees) *during the power stroke* when the exhaust valve begins to open unto the time(measured in degrees) *during the intake stroke* when the exhaust valve closes.

Exhaust stroke -- This is when the remaining burned air-fuel mixture is pushed from the cylinder as the piston moves from BDC to TDC, while the exhaust valve is open, and the intake valve is closed.

Fluid friction -- This is the friction between the air(in this case) and the intake system's (carburetor(s) and intake ports) internal surfaces that is caused by the air flowing into the cylinder.

Force -- This defined as a push or pull applied or exerted on an object.

Friction mean effective pressure -- This is the amount of mean effective pressure necessary to overcome friction in the engine.

Humidity -- This is the amount of water vapor in the air or atmosphere.

Indicated horsepower -- This is the total horsepower developed in the engine, neglecting any power losses due to friction, etc.

Indicated mean effective pressure -- See "mean effective pressure"

GLOSSARY

Intake closing time(I C) -- This is the time(in degrees) when the intake valve closes at the end of the intake phase(during the compression stroke).

Intake lobe centerline(Intake lobe ctr) -- It is the angle at which maximum valve lift occurs on the intake lobe.

Intake opening time(I O) -- This is thee time(in degrees) when the intake valve opens at the beginning of the intake phase(during the exhaust stroke).

Intake phase -- The time(measured in degrees) *during the exhaust stroke* when the intake valve begins to open unto the time(measured in degrees) *during the compression stroke* when the intake valve closes

Intake stroke -- This is when air and fuel are drawn into the cylinder as the piston moves from TDC to BDC, while the intake valve is open and the exhaust valve is closed.

Linear -- It means *straight* or action taking place *along a straight line*.

Loaded tire radius -- The radius of a tire on a car when it is in motion.

Mass -- A combined quantity of matter.

Mean effective pressure -- This is the a constant pressure that can be thought of or envisioned to be applied during the duration of the power stroke.

Minus sign(-) -- see "negative sign"

Negative sign(-) -- It indicates that a value is a negative number, and that it is decreasing.

Net air mass efficiency(Net AME) -- This is a reduction in the *"theoretical air mass efficiency"* due to the relative humidity.

One horsepower -- It is equal to 550 foot pounds of work per second*(550 ft-lbf/sec)* or 33,000 foot pounds of work per minute*(33,000 ft-lbf/min)*.

Overall gear ratio -- The transmission's gear ratio <u>times</u> the rear end gear ratio.

Overdrive -- This is when the engine's or flywheel's speed(rpm) is less than the transmission's output shaft speed(rpm). This ratio is numerically less than 1.00:1.

Partial pressure -- This is the pressure that is exerted by an element in a mixture such as *air*, or <u>*water-vapor*</u> in a mixture of *"air & <u>water-vapor</u>"*.

Positive sign(+) -- It indicates that a value is a *positive number*, and that it is increasing.

Power -- This is the rate at which work is done, or either, an amount of work done divided by the time taken to perform it.

GLOSSARY

Power phase -- This is the time(measured in degrees) *during the compression stroke* when ignition of the air-fuel mixture takes place and the intake & exhaust valves are closed, unto the time(measured in degrees) *during the power stroke* when the exhaust valve opens.

Power(expansion) stroke -- This is when the air-fuel mixture is burning and the piston is forced down from TDC to BDC, with both the intake and exhaust valves being closed.

Pressure -- This is the amount of force exerted per unit area(per square inch or square foot in this case) on a surface.

Relative humidity -- This is the ratio of the partial pressure of the water-vapor, in a mixture of air & water-vapor, to the saturation pressure of water at the same dry bulb temperature.

Revolutions per minute -- This is the number of full revolutions that a rotating object such as a crankshaft, transmission's input and/or output shaft, etc., completes in one minute.

RTF(Gear) -- This is the rear tire force exerted on the ground *in a particular gear*.

Saturation pressure(GP) -- This is the pressure at which vaporization takes place at a given temperature.

Speed -- The distance a car or object travels divided by the time it takes to travel the same distance.

Suction -- Negative pressure

Static compression ratio -- This is the ratio of the volume that is above the piston at bottom dead center to the volume that is above the piston at top dead center.

Static loaded tire radius -- This is the measured radius of a tire or tires on a vehicle while it is sitting firmly on a hard surface.

Stroke -- The distance traveled by the centerline of the crankshaft's crankpin when the piston travels from top dead center to bottom dead center.

Swept volume -- This is the volume that is displaced or remains above the piston after it travels from TDC to BDC or through one stroke of the crankshaft.

Theoretical mass efficiency -- This is the gross air mass efficiency when neglecting any losses due to humidity(water-vapor), and fluid friction.

Theoretical air mass -- The theoretical or calculated mass of air that could be taken into the cylinder under atmospheric or ambient conditions.

Time -- A non spatial infinite(non ending) span in which events or actions occur.

Tire radius -- A tire's diameter divide by two(2).

GLOSSARY

Top dead center(TDC) -- This is when the piston has reached its highest point in the cylinder.

Torque -- A force applied on a rigid body at a perpendicular distance from a given point, and that has a tendency to cause a rotation about the same point.

Underdriven -- This is when the engine's or flywheel's speed(rpm) is greater than the transmission's output shaft speed(rpm). This ratio is numerically greater than 1.00:1.

Valve timing diagram -- A diagram that shows the opening and closing points and periods of the intake and exhaust valves.

Vapor pressure(VP) -- The pressure exerted by the vapor(in this case) in an "air & water-vapor" mixture.

Velocity -- It is the speed and the direction of travel.

Volumetric efficiency -- See "air mass efficiency"

Weight -- The force of gravity exerted by the earth on an object.

Wide open throttle(WOT) -- This is when the throttle plates in a carburetor or throttle body are completely open.

Work -- The distance an object is displaced or moved, times the force that causes this displacement or movement.